SETTLERS OF RENSSELAERSWYCK
1630-1658

Edited by

A. J. F. VAN LAER

Excerpted from

THE VAN RENSSELAER BOWIER MANUSCRIPTS

with

Index to Biographical Notices

CLEARFIELD

Reprinted for
Clearfield Company, Inc. by
Genealogical Publishing Co., Inc.
Baltimore, Maryland
1998

Originally Published: Albany, New York, 1908
Reprinted: Genealogical Publishing Co., Inc.
Baltimore, 1965, 1980
Library of Congress Catalogue Card Number 65-29272
International Standard Book Number 0-8063-0359-X
Made in the United States of America

SETTLERS OF RENSSELAERSWYCK

1630–1658

This list gives a concise record of the arrival and occupation of settlers in the colony, from the date of its founding to the end of the administration of Jan Baptist van Rensselaer, in so far as such record appears in the *Van Rensselaer Bowier Manuscripts* and the *Rensselaerswyck Manuscripts*. As to the first of these sources, the statements have been limited to leading facts and the reader is referred for further information to the preceding pages of the present volume. As to the second source, a careful examination has been made of ledger accounts with colonists, 1634–77, 13 v.; accounts of Jeremias van Rensselaer, 1654–59, 1 v.; court proceedings, 1648–52, 1 v.; resolutions of the commissioners of the colony, 1652–64, 1 v.; leases and contracts, 1648–52, 1 v.; deeds, powers of attorney, etc., 1660–65, 1 v.; and a considerable number of miscellaneous papers. Together, these include practically everything of consequence that has been preserved of the early records of the colony, and the information contained therein has been given as fully and definitely as possible.

The arrangement is alphabetical under the date of arrival when known, otherwise under the date of the first entry in the accounts. Pains have been taken to indicate various forms of names and also to locate the places from which settlers came. To emphasize that the proper name preceded by *van* was a place name and not a family name, the word *van* has been translated *from* in all cases where the entries in the records made it certain that such was the case; in names, such as *van Vechten* and *van Voorhout*, which are constantly used by different members of the family and where there might be some doubt as to whether they referred to the actual place of origin or had already become family names before the persons using them left Holland, it has seemed advisable to retain the *van*. Names marked with an * are those of people who entered into contracts with the patroon, but for one reason or another did not come to the colony.

1630

By de Eendracht

Sailed from the Texel, March 21, 1630; arrived at New Amsterdam, May 24, 1630

Claes Claesz, from Vlecker [Fleckerö, an island off the south coast of Norway]; sailed with Roelof Jansz in 1630 and served as farm hand on de Laets Burg. His name does not appear in the records of the colony after 1634.

Wolfert Gerritsz, from Amersfoort; occasionally referred to as *Wolfert Gerritsz van Couwenhoven*, Couwenhoven being a farm or estate about four miles northwest of Amersfoort, in the province of Utrecht. He was engaged by the patroon in Jan. 1630 to superintend the establishment of farms in the colony and to purchase cattle. He was to serve for four years, each year from April to November, but at his request was released by the patroon in 1632. He lived at the Manhatans.

Jacob Goyversen (Goyverttsen), from Vlecker [Fleckerö, Norway]; sailed with Roelof Jansz in 1630.

Pieter Hendricksz, from Soest, [presumably the village of that name in the province of Utrecht, but possibly the city of Soest in Westphalia]; was engaged in 1630 as a shepherd or plow boy, for the term of four years, at f15 a year. He served under Rutger Hendricksz and probably left the colony in 1634.

Rutger Hendricksz, from Soest; was engaged in 1630, for four years, at f120 a year, and in 1632 appears as farmer on Rensselaers Burg, on Castle Island. He was appointed schout in 1632, but probably never qualified and seems to have left the colony in 1634.

5

Barent (Beerent) Jansz; given in one list as from *Desens,* and in another as from *Esen,* neither of which place names can be definitely indentified. He sailed in 1630 as farm servant to Brant Peelen. His name does not appear in the records of the colony after 1634.

Roelof Jansz, from Masterland [Marstrand, on the coast of Sweden]; sailed in 1630 with his wife Annetje Jans,' his daughters Sara and Trijntje and another child born before in New Netherland. He was farmer on de Laets Burg and was appointed schepen July 1, 1632. He probably left the colony in 1634.

Seger (Zeeger) Jansz, from Nykerck, [province of Gelderland]; sailed in 1630 and served as farm hand under Rutger Hendricksz, on Rensselaers Burg. Oct. 3, 1636, he is referred to as having been drowned.

Brant Peelen, from Nykerck, [province of Gelderland]; was engaged as farmer in Jan. 1630, for the term of four years, at wages of f110 a year, and in 1632 was appointed schepen. He was married twice, first to Lubbertje Wouters, by whom he had three children, Lysbeth Brants, Geert Brants and Gerritje Brants and secondly, at New Amsterdam, July 3, 1643, to Marritje Pieters, widow of Claes Sybrantsz, who had two children, Sybrant Claesz and Aeltje Claes. Lysbeth and Gerritje Brants came to the colony by den Waterhondt in 1640. One of them married Claes Jansz Calff. Brant Peelen died before May 1, 1644, when Cornelis Segersz van Voorhout succeeded him on his farm, called Welys Burg, on Castle Island.

1631

By de Eendracht
Sailed from the Texel shortly after July 7, 1631

Marinus Adriaensz (Marijn Adriaensz, Maryn Adriaensen, Marin Adriaensz, Marinus Ariaens), from Veere, [in the province of Zealand]; entered into a contract with Kiliaen van Rensselaer, Jan. 12, 1631, to serve as tobacco planter for the period of three years, if possible, on the farm on the north side of Fort Orange, "which he began to clear before his depar-' ture." He sailed with his wife Lysbet Thysen and one child and several farm laborers by de Eendracht in July 1631. In 1632 he was appointed schepen and the same year he is referred to as farmer on Godyns Burg situated south of Fort Orange. His name does not occur in the account books of the colony; he probably left the colony at the end of his term in 1634.

*Claes Brunsteyn, from Straelsundt [Stralsund, in Pomerania]; entered into an agreement with Marinus Adriaensz, May 27, 1631, but did not sail for the colony.

*Andries Christensz, from Flecker [Fleckerö, Norway]; entered into a contract with the patroon for the erection of a sawmill, July 2, 1631, but did not come to the colony.

Jasper Ferlyn (Ferlin, Ferlijn) van der Gouw, from Middelburgh, [in the province of Zealand]; entered the service of Marinus Adriaensz as tobacco planter, Feb. 17, 1631, for the term of three years, beginning on his arrival in the colony. His name does not appear in the account books of the colony; he probably left at the end of his term in 1634.

* Cornelis Goverts (Gerritssz), from Flecker [Fleckerö, Norway]; was engaged to sail by de Eendracht in 1631, but failed to go.

Laurens Laurensz (Lourenssen, Loerens), from Coppenhagen; also referred to as *Laurens Laurensen noorman*. He and two other Scandinavians were engaged, July 2, 1631, for three years, to erect a sawmill in the colony. Laurens Laurensz was appointed schepen in 1632 and in July of that year is referred to by the patroon as miller on de Laets kil, which is the present Mill Creek in the city of Rensselaer. Laurens Laurensz' name does not appear in the business accounts of the colony for 1634; he probably left at the end of his term of service.

Cornelis Maesen (Maersz, Maertsz, Martsen, Maessen), from Buyrmalsen [Buurmalsem, in the province of Gelderland]; sailed for New Netherland as a farm laborer in 1631, having been engaged by the patroon on May 27th, for the term of three years, and went back to Holland shortly after Aug. 2, 1634, on which date he is charged in the colony with f12:18 for clothes and brandy. Aug. 15, 1636, he entered into a new contract with the patroon and the same year he sailed by the Rensselaerswyck, accompanied by his wife Catelijntje Martens and a servant by the name of Cornelis Teunisz, from Westbroeck. On the voyage, Jan. 30, 1637, a son was born named Hendrick Cornelisz. Cornelis: Maesen arrived in the colony the second time about April 17, 1637. From that time till his death, some time before April 8, 1648, he occupied a farm on or near Papscanee Island. Cornelis Maesen and his wife were buried the same day; their effects were sold at auction Shrove Tuesday, 1649.

Barent Thonisz (Berent Thonis, Thonissen, Tonisz, Theunisz, Thomassen), from Heijligesont [Hellesund, on the south coast of Norway]; he and two other Scandinavians were engaged, July 2, 1631, for the period of three years, to build a sawmill in the colony. The name of Barent Thonisz does not appear in the account books of the colony; he probably left at the end of his term in 1634.

Jan Tyaerts (Thyerts, Chierts, Teersz, Terssen, Treersz), from Franicker, [in the province of Friesland]; was engaged as a farm laborer, May 27, 1631, for the period of three years, at f60 a year, and sailed with Marinus Adriaensz on de Eendracht in July of that year. In the account books he is entered as a farm hand of Cornelis Teunisz, from Breuckelen, from June 1, 1635, to July 19, 1637. He probably left the colony soon after the last named date.

1633

By den Soutberg

Sailed from the Texel shortly after July 20, 1632; arrived at New Amsterdam in April 1633

Hendrick Fredericksz (Frerixsen), from Bunnick, [near Utrecht]; was engaged as farm laborer for Gerrit Theusz de Reux and sailed with him, being then 26 years of age. In the accounts of the colony he is charged with supplies from 1638 to 1643 and credited with wages earned in cutting straw, thatching roofs, threshing and other work, between 1638 and 1650. In May 1638, he acted as foreman on de Reux' farm.

Cornelis Jacobsz, from Martensdyck, [near Utrecht]; was engaged as farm laborer for Rutger. Hendricksz, on Rensselaers Burg and sailed with Gerrit Theusz de Reux, being then 23 years of age. His name does not appear in the account books of the colony.

Marcus Mensen (Mens, Meussen), from Culenburgh, or Cuylenborch, [province of Gelderland]; was engaged as farm boy for Brant Peelen, on Welys Burg, and sailed with Gerrit Theusz de Reux, being then 17 years of age. The entries of his account in the colony, April 17–Aug. 18, 1637, are canceled.

Gerrit Theusz de Reux (de Reus); was engaged by the patroon as farmer on a farm to be established on Blommaerts kil, June 15, 1632, but had previously been in charge of a farm of the West India Company on the island of Manhattan. He sailed with four farm laborers by den Soutberg, which brought Wouter van Twiller to New Netherland. Before sailing, de Reux was appointed schepen of the colony. In April 1634, he had succeeded Roelof Jansz, from Masterland, on de Laets Burg. He died before Aug. 4, 1639.

Cornelis Teunisz, from Meerkerck, [province of South Holland]; was engaged as farm laborer for Gerrit Theusz de Reux and sailed with him, being then 20 years of age. His first account in the colony runs from Feb. 2 to Aug. 20, 1637; he next appears in 1640, and later is said to have come on den Harinck; presumably therefore, he visited Holland shortly after Aug. 20, 1637, and returned to the colony by den Harinck in 1639. He is charged with three years' hire of two horses from 1640 to 1643, and credited with wages earned in cutting and hauling timber. His name does not appear in the records of the colony after 1643.

1634

By de Eendracht
Sailed from the Texel in the beginning of May 1634

Hendrick Carstensz, from Norden, [East Friesland]; sailed by de Eendracht and served under Brant Peelen from July 20, 1634, for four years, at f25 a year, and again for three years, at f140 a year. He does not appear in the records of the colony after 1643.

* Hendrick Conduit, from Coninghsbergen [Königsberg, East Prussia]; made a contract with the patroon on April 15, 1634, but failed to come to the colony.

Lubbert Gijsbertsz, from Blaricum, [near Naarden, in the province of North Holland], wheelwright; made a contract with the patroon on April 15, 1634, and sailed with his wife Divertgen Cornelis and three sons, Gijsbert, Theus and Jan, by de Eendracht. His account in the colony runs from July 20, 1634 to 1647.

Robbert Hendricksz; is credited in the accounts with wages at f11 a month, from Dec. 16, 1634, to June 23, 1635; with f30 for splitting 3500 *pallesaeten* (stockade posts) for the farm on Castle Island; and with f62:8 for splitting 5000 similar posts for the new farm of Cornelis Teunisz. His account was closed June 23, 1635.

Jan Jacobsz; credited with 13½ months' wages at f11 a month for service as farm hand under Brant Peelen on Castle Island, with f100 for threshing and with 12 months' wages at f13 a month. His service ended apparently April 17, 1637.

Jacob Albertsz Planck, from Edam, [province of North Holland]; bound himself, March 4, 1634, to serve as schout and agent of the colony for three years from the date of his arrival and sailed with his son Abraham Jacobsz Planck and one servant by de Eendracht. In a letter of Oct. 3, 1636, he is called " officer and *commis.*" Planck's accounts run from Aug. 12, 1634, to Nov. 26, 1637, but apparently he did not leave Rensselaerswyck till after van Curler's arrival in 1638. Sept. 20, 1639, he certified at Amsterdam to the sale of Papscanee Island by the Indians, on April 23, 1637. Planck was the second person to receive an appointment as schout, Rutger Hendricksz, from Soest, having been appointed as such in July 1632, but in all probability Planck was the first schout who took the oath and held court.

Cornelis Anthonisz van Schlick, from Breuckelen, [near Utrecht]; generally referred to as *Cornelis Teunisz,* often as *Broer Cornelis* and occasionally as *Cornelis Teunisz, alias Broeder;* signs his name *Cornelis anthonnisen van schlick.* He was a carpenter and mason and sailed by de Eendracht in 1634, having entered into a contract with the patroon on April 5th of that year. His account in the colony begins Aug. 12, 1634. He was before Oct. 1636 in charge of a farm, which till 1648 he seems to have worked on shares; from 1648 to 1652 he is charged·with an annual rent of f600; from 1652 to 1661, with an annual rent of f500. The indications are that during all these years he occupied the same farm, which appears to have been located some distance north of the fifth, now Patroon's, creek and to have adjoined the farm called de Vlackte, later known as the Schuyler Flatts. Between 1643 and 1648, Cornelis Teunisz spent much of his time at the Manhatans; Aug. 6, 1646, de Hooges urges him to come up the river to see how the harvest proceeds and intimates that he might come to the colony at least once a year to look after his farm. While at the Manhatans, Aug. 22, 1646, he received from Director Kieft a patent for land at Catskill, in return for services rendered in bringing about general peace and in ransoming prisoners in the hands of the Indians. He was appointed the patroon's *voorspraecke,* or representative, May 12, 1639, and as such filled the place of officer jointly with Arent van Curler and Pieter Cornelisz, till the arrival of van der Donck in 1641. Sept. 23, 1650, he was chosen to go with van Curler and others on an embassy to the Maquaes, and in 1658, 1660 and 1661 he was a member of the court of the colony.

1637

By the Rensselaerswyck

Sailed from the Texel, October 8, 1636; arrived at New Amsterdam, March 4, 1637

Albert Andriesz, from Frederikstad, [in the southeast of Norway]; hence, in the early records, his designation as *Noorman.* After 1670, he became known as *Albert Andriesz Bradt.* Aug. 26, 1636, he joined Pieter Cornelisz and Claes Jansz in an agreement with the patroon for the erection of a mill in the colony. In this agreement he is given as tobacco planter, 29 years of age. He sailed with his wife Annetje Barents on the Rensselaerswyck, Oct. 8, 1636, and appears first in the colony under date of April 17, 1637. Soon after his arrival he left Pieter Cornelisz and established himself as tobacco planter. From May 4, 1652, to May 4, 1672, he is charged with an annual rent of f250 for two mills and land on the Normans Kill. Annetje Barents died before June 5, 1662, leaving him eight children of whom the eldest was born on the Rensselaerswyck and named *Storm.* This son later adopted the name of *van der Zee.* Albert Andriesz married the second time Geertruy Pietersz Vosburgh. He is said to have died June 7, 1686.

Arent Andriesz, tobacco planter; a brother of Albert Andriesz, from Frederikstad, and like him designated as *Noorman.* He appears to have come over with his brother on the Rensselaerswyck and to have stayed with him in the colony for one year. His wages began April 2, 1637, at f75 a year. Between 1638 and 1646, he is various times credited with tobacco furnished to van Curler and de Hooges. May 1, 1658, he obtained a lease for land opposite Beverwyck.

Thijs Barentsz, shoemaker; charged with supplies from June 5, 1637, to 1643, when he was indebted to the amount of f341:14. Jan. 18, 1652, he was ordered to pay his account within a month.

Maurits Jansz van Broeckhuysen; was a young relative of Kiliaen van Rensselaer and came out as farm hand by the Rensselaerswyck. May 12, 1639, he was authorized to establish himself as farmer on de Laets Burg, on the farm formerly occupied by Gerrit Theusz de Reux. In the accounts he is credited with four years' salary, at f110 a year, beginning April 3, 1637. One half year's wages are charged to Cornelis Teunisz, from Breuckelen. His account closes Sept. 7, 1641. Feb. 12, 1642, he is referred to by Kiliaen van Rensselaer as having lately returned from New Netherland.

Carsten Carstensz (Christen Christensz), commonly referred to as *Carsten Carstensz Noorman;* is first entered in the accounts under date of April 17, 1637, hence probably came on the Rensselaerswyck. Before 1644, he was employed as a farm laborer, sawyer, stave splitter, mill hand and roof thatcher. Afterwards he leased a garden, which in 1650 was granted to Gijsbert Cornelisz, from Weesp.

Gijsbert Claesz, also referred to as *Gijsbert Claesz Jongen* (the boy); was a carpenter by trade and like Jacob Jansz, from Amsterdam, is credited in the accounts with four years' wages from April 2, 1637, at f40 a year. Both men appear to have been employed by Albert Andriesz and probably came over with him on the Rensselaerswyck. His account closes Sept. 5, 1641.

Pieter Claesz (Niclaesz), from Nordingen, or Norden, [in East Friesland]; is credited with six years' wages from April 3, 1637, and in Aug. 1644 is mentioned as servant of Symon Walichsz. He probably arrived with the latter on the Rensselaerswyck. He is charged with rent, at f11 a year, from 1643 to 1645, and in 1648–49 appears to have occupied a farm at Bethlehem. He left the colony before June 5, 1649. He was the son in law of Cornelis Hendricksz van Nes.

Crijn (Quirijn) Cornelisz, from Houten, [near Utrecht]. His accounts in the colony run from April 20, 1637, to Aug. 21, 1639 and from Jan 1, 1641, to 1648. May 30, 1640, he is referred to by the patroon as about to sail from Holland. Presumably, therefore, he came out on the Rensselaerswyck in 1637, went back to Holland in 1639 and returned to the colony by den Waterhondt in 1640, accompanied by Cornelis Crijnen, Jan Crijnen, Jan Cornelisz and Jan Reyersz, all from Houten. He served at first under Gerrit

Theusz de Reux and from Jan. 1, 1641, to Jan. 1, 1642, as farm hand on a farm in Greenbush, which he thereafter seems to have occupied as farmer, jointly with Pieter Teunisz, from Brunswijck. In April 1648, he was repeatedly ordered to settle his accounts and Nov. 18, 1649, his farm was leased to Evert Pels and Willem Fredericksz [Bout]. With Christoffel Davids, he also occupied, till stubble time 1649, six morgens of land in Greenbush, which in 1650 were leased to Teunis Dircksz van Vechten. Nov. 2, 1651, Crijn Cornelisz and Hans Jansz, from Rotterdam, received permission to erect a sawmill on a creek on the west side of the river, a little north of Beeren Island.

Pieter Cornelisz, from Munnickendam, [in the province of North Holland]; occasionally referred to as Pieter Cornelisz Meulenmaecker (mill wright); sailed by the Rensselaerswyck, Sept. 25, 1636, after having entered in company with Claes Jansz, from Naerden, and Albert Andriesz, from Frederikstad, into an agreement with the patroon for the erection of a sawmill in the colony. In this agreement, dated Aug. 26, 1636, his age is given as 43 years. His account in the colony begins May 4, 1637, and closes May 3, 1649, but from the log of the Rensselaerswyck he is known to have sailed up the river as early as March 24, 1637, and from other documents it would seem that he left the colony in 1646. Oct. 3, 1636, he was appointed councilor and schepen, and May 12, 1639, he received a commission as receiver of tithes and supercargo of the colony's vessel. Jan. 31, 1646, Pieter Cornelisz made a contract with Antony de Hooges for building a horsepower mill in Greenbush, the mill on the fifth creek being most of the time out of order and too inconvenient for the inhabitants on account of *het heen en wedervaeren* (the sailing back and forth).

Roelof Cornelisz, from Houten, [near Utrecht]; brother of Crijn Cornelisz, from Houten; is charged with supplies furnished to him in 1638 and may have arrived with Crijn Cornelisz in 1637. He was at various times employed in splitting wood and in thatching roofs of houses and in 1646 is charged with hire of horses and cows and rent of land.

Goossen Gerritsz, from Westerbroeck [Westbroek, province of Utrecht?]; was engaged for six years, three years at f50 a year and three years at f80 a year. His wages in the colony began April 8, 1637; he probably came by the Rensselaerswyck. In 1646, he is charged with f19:9 received in Holland on Nov. 3, 1645. In Oct. 1648, on the repeated solicitation by the director to accept the place of *gerechts persoon* (member of the court), he pleaded to be excused on the ground that he did not consider himself fit for the office, that he was not possessed of a house and lot and therefore not bound to serve, and that he had not yet settled all his accounts with the patroon. His objections however were overruled and he was urged once more to accept the office, the court, in case of refusal, threatening to proceed to other measures. He finally yielded, on condition that he be first allowed to make a trip to the Manhatans. This was granted and Nov. 19, 1648, he took the oath as member of the court. At his urgent request he was released from his office on Jan. 5, 1651. In the accounts he is charged from 1648 to 1652 with f32 a year for ground rent of a house and license to trade and, jointly with Rutger Jacobsz, from May 1649 to May 1650 with f450 for the lease of the brewery. July 18, 1650, he was granted permission to become a tapster and Sept. 9, 1650, he was with Arent van Curler appointed trustee of a fund for the building of a school. From May 1, 1655, to May 1, 1658, he and Thomas Jansz are charged with an annual rent of f40, for a small piece of land situated opposite *den sack*. July 19, [1659?] he entered into an agreement with Jeremias van Rensselaer regarding the purchase of hides of cattle to be killed in the colony, showing that by that time he was engaged in the tanning business. After 1660, he is occasionally referred to as *Goossen Gerritsz van Schaick.*

Robert Harmensz; his account in the colony runs from April 17, 1637, to 1638. He is credited with wages earned in repairing a fence, splitting wood, thatching and grinding, and would seem to have been in the employ of Gerrit de Reux. He came probably by the Rensselaerswyck.

Adriaen Huybertsz; is credited with six years' wages at f100 a year, from April 8, 1637; like others whose term of service began at that date, he came probably by the Rensselaerswyck. For four and one half years he was employed by Cornelis Teunisz, from Breuckelen. In 1652, he is charged with five years' rent, at f300 a year, for a farm on the fifth creek, which he seems to have taken over from Rutger Jacobsz, and for the same length of time with f20 a year for trading privileges.

Rutger (Ruth) Jacobsz, from Schoonderwoert [Schoonrewoerd, province of South Holland]; served as farm hand on the farm of Cornelis Teunisz, from Breuckelen, for the term of six years, beginning April 8, 1637, at f100 a year, and probably came on the Rensselaerswyck. Feb. 9, 1643, he was engaged as foreman on *de groote Vlacte* (the great Flats) at f220 a year, a suit of clothes, two shirts and two pairs of shoes, his term of service to begin April 7, 1643. From Jan. 1, 1645, he appears as lessee of a farm on the fifth creek, which in 1647 seems to have been taken over by Adriaen Huybertsz. From 1648 to 1654 he is charged with an annual rent of f125 for a sawmill on the fifth creek, taken over from Andries de Vos, and for the same period he is charged, jointly with Barent Pietersz, with an annual rent of f550 for a saw- and grist-mill, also on the fifth creek. He owned a yacht from about 1648, and April 4, 1649, agreed to pay f32 a year, for three years, for rent of his house lot and the right to the fur trade. Oct. 18, 1650, he and Goossen Gerritsz were authorized to brew beer, on condition of paying a duty of one guilder for every barrel of beer and of brewing, free of charge, the beer needed for the households of van Slichtenhorst and de Hooges. Rutger Jacobsz is credited with f36 for nine months' salary as *raets vriendt* (councilor) and again with salary as councilor, at the rate of f50 a year, from Dec. 18, 1649, to Oct. 18, 1651, when at his urgent request he was released from his duties and succeeded by Jan Baptist van Rensselaer. Rutger Jacobsz married June 3, 1646, at New Amsterdam, Trijntje Jans, from *Breestede* [Bredstedt, in Schleswig], and died before Dec. 9, 1665.

Claes Jansz, from Nykerck, [province of Gelderland]; is credited with four years' wages, at f120 a year, beginning April 2, 1637, and with carpenter work done between 1642 and 1644 on houses of van Curler, van der Donck, Megapolensis and others. Aug. 30, 1646, Antony de Hooges ordered Nicolaes Coorn, officer of the colony, to seize grain on the farm of Broer Cornelis and to turn the same over to Claes Jansz, from Nykerck, in payment of wages earned by him on de Vlackte while Broer Cornelis was at the Manhatans, as per account of Ruth Jacobsz.

Dirck Jansz, from Edam, [in the province of North Holland]. He and Reynier Thijmensz, from Edam, entered into a contract with Kiliaen van Rensselaer on Aug. 26, 1636, to sail by the ship Rensselaerswyck and to settle in the colony as free colonists, for a period of four years. He is charged in the accounts with supplies from May 9, 1637, to 1642. Under date of May 29, 1643, he is referred to as deceased. He was a member of the council of the colony in 1637.

Jacob Jansz, from Amsterdam; was a carpenter by trade and was engaged for the term of four years, beginning April 2, 1637, at wages of f40 a year. He appears for part of this period to have been employed by Albert Andriesz; in the harvest of 1640, he served under Cornelis Teunisz, from Breuckelen. May 1, 1640, he received f32 extra pay for " faithful service to the patroon." In 1641 he was employed by van Curler to do some copying and from that date till Aug. 20, 1643, when his account was closed by van Curler, he was engaged with other carpenters in building houses and barns.

Thomas Jansz, from Bunnick, [near Utrecht]; was engaged as farm hand for the term of six years, beginning April 8, 1637, at f110 a year, and served under Brant Peelen and Symon Walichsz. He probably came by the Rensselaerswyck. From May 1, 1646, to 1650 he occupied a farm, for which he is charged with an annual rent first of f180 and then of f130; April 11, 1650, van Slichtenhorst leased to him an additional piece of land formerly occupied by Hendrick Albertsz, and from that time till 1652 he is charged with rent of f180 a year. From May 1, 1655, to May 1, 1658, he and Goossen Gerritsz are charged with rent and tithes for a small parcel of land on the east side of the river opposite *den sack*.

In 1656, the accounts contain the name of *Thomas jansen Timmerman*. This man is probably to be identified with Thomas Jansz Mingael, the carpenter, who appears to have been a resident of Beverwyck, and not a settler of Rensselaerswyck.

Jean Labatie (Lebatie, Lebattij, Labatyn, Labatis), also referred to as *Johan Labatie fransman* (Frenchman); was engaged as a journeyman carpenter for the term of four years, beginning April 2, 1637, at f80 a year, and for part of the time was employed by Albert Andriesz. At the end of the four years, he engaged himself to the patroon for three years more, at f200 a year. Thereafter, van Curler intended to put him on the farm at the Great Flats to trade, but he probably left the patroon's service. In 1648, he is charged in the accounts with the patroon's *Gerechticheyt* (dues) for four years, beginning May 1, 1643, compounded at the rate of f25 a year, which may indicate that he was engaged in the Indian trade, as in 1650 he is spoken of as being well versed in the Maquaes language. June 15, 1647, he received permission from the West India company to erect a house in Fort Orange and to brew therein; in 1649, he is referred to by van Slichtenhorst as being in command of the fort, which may have reference to a temporary absence of Carel van Brugge, who was appointed *commis* Nov. 6, 1647, and is supposed to have acted in that capacity till 1651. Sept. 23, 1650. Jean Labatie, inhabitant of Fort Orange, was summoned to the house of Director van Slichtenhorst and asked to accompany van Curler, Cornelis Teunisz, from Breuckelen, Thomas Chambers and Volckert Hansz on an embassy to the Maquaes to renew the covenant of friendship, but he refused to go, saying that it made little difference to those in the fort whether they were at war or at peace with the Indians. Aug. 26, 1652, Labatie and Cornelis Teunisz, from Breuckelen, jointly leased the farm formerly occupied by Cornelis Teunisz, but in the accounts Labatie is not charged with rent for this farm and it is likely that he never occupied it. July 20, 1654, Labatie took over the farm on Castle Island formerly leased to Jan Barentsz Wemp, for which from stubble time 1654 to May 1, 1655, he is charged with f150 and thereafter with an annual rent of f300. Feb. 20, 1672, Labatie settled his accounts with Jeremias van Rensselaer.

Arent Pietersz, generally referred to as *Arent Pietersz Jongen* (the boy); was engaged for six years, beginning April 3, 1637, three years at f45 and three years at f75 a year, and served at different times under Albert Andriesz, Cornelis Teunisz and Teunis Dircksz. He is probably the same person as *Aert Pietersz alias Solder*, or *Solder Pietersz*, who was furnished with supplies in 1642 and who appears as late as 1651. The nickname *Solder* would seem to indicate that he was in charge of a *graan zolder*, that is, a grain loft, or granary. July 8, 1649, *Aert Pietersz* was summoned before the court to state whether he would fulfil his promise to *seecker vrouwmens, genaemt Blancke ael* (a certain woman, called fair Alida) and in reply declared that he would marry her at the first opportunity.

Jacob Pietersz, from Utrecht; in one account referred to as *Jacob Pietersz van Uijtrecht alias Veeltje*, and in another as *Jacob Pietersz Veeltje;* was engaged for six years, from April 8, 1637, at f100 a year, and served under Brant Peelen. He left the colony on, or before, Nov. 16, 1644.

* **Hans van Sevenhuysen**; sailed by the Rensselaerswyck as smith's helper to Cornelis Thomasz, but was arrested in England for killing his master in a tavern at Ilfracombe, Dec. 8, 1636.

Arent Steffeniersz (Steevenniersz, Steveniersen), hog dealer; entered into a contract with Kiliaen van Rensselaer before Oct. 4, 1636, and sailed by the Rensselaerswyck. March 22, 1637, he married at the Manhatans the widow of the murdered smith, Cornelis Thomasz. Arent Steffeniersz is charged with supplies in the colony from April 17, 1637, to 1644. In 1639, he accompanied Pieter Cornelisz, from Munnickendam, to the Manhatans to get lime and iron.

Cornelis Teunisz, from Westbroeck (Westerbroeck, Wesbroeck, Wijsbroeck); also referred to as *Cornelis Theunisz bos, Cornelis Theunisz vanden bos, Cornelis Theunissen schoester*, and *Kees schoester;* signs his name *Cornelis thonisen bos*. He came probably from the village of Westbroek, in the province of Utrecht, and would seem from the designation *schoester*, to have been a shoemaker by trade. He sailed with Cornelis Maesen by the Rensselaerswyck, in 1636, and served him in the colony for six years, beginning April 8, 1637, at wages of f100 a year. As early as April 8, 1648, he and Teunis Dircksz van Vechten are mentioned as guardians of the minor children of the late Cornelis Maesen. March 25, 1649, Cornelis Teunisz, from Westbroeck, Volckert Hansz and Cornelis Vos were warned not to engage in illicit trade with the Indians; April 3, 1649, their license was revoked for not observing the ordinance. July 13, 1650, Cornelis Teunisz was ordered to send Jan Hagemans, a free trader, away from his house; April 1, 1650, he was granted the use of a garden between the first and second creeks. He was a magistrate of Fort Orange, prior to Aug. 19, 1662.

Reynier Thijmensz (Tijmense, Timansz, Tymansen), from Edam, [province of North Holland]. He and Dirck Jansz, from Edam, entered into a contract with Kiliaen van Rensselaer, Aug. 26, 1636, to sail by the Rensselaerswyck and to settle in the colony as free colonists for the period of four years. His account in the colony begins May 7, 1637, and closes Sept. 12, 1643. In an extract from his contract his name is given as *reijnier thomassen.*

* **Cornelis Thomasz,** from Rotterdam; engaged as smith, Oct. 4, 1636, and sailed with his wife by the Rensselaerswyck. Dec. 8, 1636, he was stabbed to death by his helper, Hans van Sevenhuysen, in a tavern at Ilfracombe. His widow was married to Arent Steffeniersz, March 22, 1637, at New Amsterdam. Burger Jorisz took his place as smith of the colony.

Teunis Cornelisz van Vechten; his first account in the colony, entered under the name of *theunis Cornelissen van der vechten Jongen,* runs from April 8 to Nov. 14, 1637. He appears next in 1641 as having been three years in the service of Michiel Jansz. It is not unlikely therefore that he arrived as a boy, on the Rensselaerswyck, early in 1637, went back to Holland in the winter of that year, and returned to the colony in 1638, with Michiel Jansz and Teunis Dircksz van Vechten, both of whom came by het Wapen van Noorwegen. He probably came from Vechten, a small village southeast of Utrecht. In the *Schult Boeck vande goederen vant'schip den Waterhondt,* 1640–41, his name is indexed as *Teunis Cornelissen van Westbroeck,* but this is probably a clerical error, due to confusion with *Cornelis Teunisz van Westbroeck.* Between 1647 and 1656, he is referred to as *Thunis Cornelissen alias jonge Poetien, toenis Cornelisz poyntgen* and *tunis Cornelisen Jonge poentie.* Teunis Cornelisz served under Michiel Jansz till May 1, 1646, and then succeeded him on the farm called de Hoogeberch, which he occupied till May 1, 1648. Oct. 15, 1648, Director van Slichtenhorst leased to him for six years the south end of *het greenenbos* (pine woods) with six morgens of old land forming part of the farm of Teunis Dircksz van Vechten, but, owing apparently to animosity on the part of Teunis Dircksz, he was allowed to leave the farm Jan. 27, 1650, and was promised a house in some other part of the colony. Jan. 29, 1650, he complained that the house which he occupied was uninhabitable on account of smoke and Mar. 17, 1650, Director van Slichtenhorst sold to him for f125 a small house south of the fifth creek, formerly occupied by Barent Pietersz and Jan Gerritsz, deceased.

Symon Walichsz (Walichs, Walichsen, Walinchsz, Walings, Walingen, Waelingen), from Wijngaerden, [in the district of het Bildt, in the province of Friesland]; entered into a contract with the patroon Aug. 15, 1636, and sailed by the Rensselaerswyck. His account in the colony begins April 17, 1637. He occupied a farm on Papscanee Island till May 1, 1647, when it was leased to Evert Pels, for six years, at f560 a year. Jan. 14, 1649, Evert Pels had the lease transferred to Juriaen Bestval and Jochem Kettelheym. Symon Walichsz agreed to buy Pieter van der Linden's plantation on Manhattan Island, Oct. 7, 1648. and was killed by the Indians near Paulus Hook, at Pavonia, in March 1649 (*see N.Y.Col.Mss,* 4:428, where his name is given as *Sijmon Walingen vant bilt*).

Burger Jorisz; was at New Amsterdam in 1637 and was secured as smith of Rensselaerswyck to take the place of Cornelis Thomasz, who had been killed by his helper Hans van Sevenhuysen, on the voyage out, at

Ilfracombe, Dec. 8, 1636. The terms upon which Burger Jorisz was engaged are as follows: "Inasmuch as Cornelis Tomassen died and Arent Steveniersen, who married the widow, dòes not understand smith's work, the council of the colony have decided to turn the iron and coal and all the tools over to *Burger Jorisen Smit* at 50% advance in price, and to let him do the work àt the rates paid by freemen at thé Manhatans, to wit: pound work at six stivers, nails at 10 stivers a hundred, braces at 12 stivers, double braces at 28 stivers and other work proportionately, and this till the patroon makes different arrangements. In the year 1637, the 26th of May, and was signed, Jacob Albertsen Planck, Pieter Cornelissen, X the mark of Dirck Jansen." Burger Jorisz' account in the colony runs from June 4, 1637, to Aug. 18, 1639, when he turned over his tools to Reyer Stoffelsz and moved to the Manahatans. Dec. 18, 1639, he married at New Amsterdam, Engeltje Mans, from Sweden. In the marriage records of the Reformed Dutch church of New York, Burger Jorisz is given as from *Hersberg, in Silesien* (Hirschberg, in Silesia).

1638

By den Harinck

Sailed from the Texel shortly after September 21, 1637; arrived at New Amsterdam, March 28, 1638

Frans Altersz (Aldersz, Albertsz), cooper; sailed by den Harinck, Sept. 1637, in the stead of Jan Willemsz Schut. His board on the ship is charged to Symon Walichsz. He is credited with wages for 39 months and 15 days, at f14 a month, beginning April 27, 1638, and is charged with supplies till 1642. Nov. 20, 1644, a bill of Frans Altersz, for cooper's work, signed by Symon Walichsz, is sent to Arent van Curler, then on his way to Holland.

Jacob Jansz (Gardenier), from Campen [Kampen, in the province of Overyssel], carpenter; generally referred to as *Jacob Jansz flodder;* appears first in the accounts of the colony as *knecht* (helper or servant) of Claes Jansz Ruyter and not unlikely sailed with him on den Harinck, in Sept. 1637. In the spring of 1642 he was at Amsterdam and applied to the patroon for permission to do carpenter work in the colony; the same year he is in the accounts charged with supplies. In 1647 he had a saw- and gristmill in Greenbush which on Nov. 18, 1649, was leased to Evert Pels and Willem Fredericksz. From 1653 to 1654 he appears as lessee of a mill at Bethlehem and Feb. 2, 1654, he obtained the lease of the saw- and gristmill on the fifth creek, for the term of eight years, beginning May 18, 1654. In the first two volumes of deeds in the Albany county clerk's office, he is referred to as *Jacob Jansz Gardenier, alias Flodder.*

Claes Jansz, from Naerden, [province of North Holland]; also referred to as *Claes Jansz Ruyter,* and as *Claes de Ruijter;* was a house carpenter by trade and 33 years of age in 1636. Aug. 26, 1636, he entered, jointly with Pieter Cornelisz and Albert Andriesz, into an agreement with the patroon for the erection of a sawmill in the colony, but for some reason failed to accompany his partners on the Rensselaerswyck in 1636, and sailed by den Harinck in Sept. 1637. In May 1640, he and his wife Pietertje Jans were apparently living at the Manhatans. He is credited in the accounts with 60 weeks' board of Arent van Curler.

By den Calmer Sleutel
Sailed from the Texel at the end of December 1637

Gijsbert Adriaensz (Arentsz, Aertsz), from Bunnick, [near Utrecht]; sailed on den Calmer Sleutel, at the age of 22, and was engaged as farm servant for six years, at wages ranging from f80 to f110 a year. He served for four years, beginning April 2, 1638, on the farm of Brant Peelen; for ¾ year on the farm of Teunis Dircksz; and for 1¼ years, jointly with Sander Leendersz, in running the colony's yacht Rensselaerswyck. He was a brother of Rutger Adriaensz, the tailor, who appears first in 1646.

Arent van Curler (Corler), from Nykerck, [in the province of Gelderland]; sailed as assistant to Jacob Albertsz Planck by den Calmer Sleutel, at the age of 18 years. May 12, 1639, he was commissioned secretary and bookkeeper of the colony, and from 1642 to 1644 he held the office of *commis*. He sailed for Holland by het Wapen van Rensselaerswyck, Oct. 20, 1644, having married, probably in 1643, Anthonia Slachboom, or Slaghboom, whom O'Callaghan, apparently on the strength of van Curler's statement, *History of New Netherland*, 1:464, has identified with Teuntje Jeuriaens, the widow of Jonas Bronck. Sept. 30, 1647, while van Curler was still in Holland, he obtained a lease for six years of the farm called de Vlackte, but May 5, 1649, this lease was transferred to Jacob Jansz, from Stoutenburch. Van Curler returned to New Netherland probably at the end of 1647 and on the arrival of Director van Slichtenhorst, early in 1648, was nominated as *Gecommitteerde*, but various circumstances prevented his accepting the office and taking the oath till Jan. 5, 1651. In the accounts he is credited with an annual salary of f200, as *Gecommitteerde & raetsvrint*, from July 1, 1652 to July 1, 1655, and with an annual salary of f200, as *gecommitteerde*, from 1655 to 1658. Sept. 9, 1650, on the petition of the inhabitants of the colony, Arent van Curler and Goossen Gerritsz were appointed trustees of voluntary contributions for the erection of a school, and Sept. 23, 1650, van Curler was chosen to go with others on an embassy to the Maquaes. He became one of the leaders in the settlement of Schenectady in 1661–62, and was drowned on Lake Champlain in 1667.

Elbert Elbertsz (Albertsz), from Nykerck, [in the province of Gelderland]; was a weaver by trade and sailed by den Calmer Sleutel, at the age of 18 years. In 1646 he married Aeltje Cornelis, the widow of Gerrit Wolphertsz (*N.Y.Col.Mss*, 2:152).

Gerrit Hendricksz, from Nykerck, [province of Gelderland], shoemaker; sailed with Arent van Curler by den Calmer Sleutel, at the age of 15 years. He was engaged for six years, at wages ranging from f40 to f100 a year; his first three years' wages, from April 2, 1638, to April 2, 1641, are charged to Albert Andriesz. He does not appear in the records of the colony after 1642.

Claes Jansz, from Nykerck, [province of Gelderland]; was a tailor by trade and sailed with Arent van Curler by den Calmer Sleutel, at the age of 17 years.

By het Wapen van Noorwegen
Sailed from the Texel in May 1638; arrived at New Amsterdam
about August 4, 1638

Adriaen Cornelisz, from Barsingerhorn, [province of North Holland]; also referred to as *Adriaen Cornelisz Berghoorn* and *Adriaen Cornelisz van Barsingerwout;* was engaged May 10, 1638, for three years, as foreman under Maurits Jansz, and sailed on het Wapen van Noorwegen. His wages in the colony, at f140 a year, began Aug. 14, 1638. He does not appear after 1643.

Jan Dircksz, from Amersfoort, [in the province of Utrecht]; is entered in the accounts as *Jan dircksen Engelsman van Amersfoort,* showing that he was a native of England; was engaged as farm laborer, for six years, at wages ranging from f30 to f50 a year. His service in the colony began Aug. 16, 1638, and he appears at first as servant of Michiel Jansz, so that he probably arrived with the latter on het Wapen van Noorwegen. In 1644, he was employed by Reyer Stoffelsz. Nov. 19, 1648, Claes Gerritsz testified that Ruth Jacobsz ordered him to beat Jan Dircksz Engelsman, if he proved refractory.

Claes Gijsbertsz; was, apparently in 1641, in the service of Michiel Jansz and may have come out with him by het Wapen van Noorwegen, in 1638.

Symon Jansz Henypot, son in law of Pieter Cornelisz, from Munnickendam; sailed by het Wapen van Noorwegen and was apparently in the colony for a short time in 1639.

Michiel Jansz, from Schrabbekercke ['s Heer Abtskerke in the province of Zealand]; came with his wife and two servants by het Wapen van Noorwegen in 1638. He was originally engaged as farm hand, but before his departure from Holland was promoted to farmer; he served as foreman in 1638 and 1639, and from 1640 to 1646 was farmer on the farm called de Hoogeberch. July 27, 1646, he received permission to leave the colony and to reside at the Manhatans, on condition that his accounts be settled. Oct. 8, 1648, the court ordered him to prepare a full statement of his accounts by Saturday next, or sooner, " if his voyage should thereby be delayed." Oct. 10, a similar order was issued and a few days later Director van Slichtenhorst asked that the court impose on Michiel Jansz the penalty of death or such other sentence as it shall see fit for the sale of ammunition to Indians during the war, together with a fine of f50 for beavers sent to Fort de Hoop, 1644, without paying duty. May 20, 1649, the court once more ordered Michiel Jansz to render a detailed account and July 27, 1650, he was asked to sign the account rendered by him.

Willem Meynten (Meijntten, Mijnten, Menten); served as a farm laborer under Cornelis Maesen for the period of six years, beginning Aug. 14, 1638, at wages ranging from f40 to f60 a year. Thereafter, he carted stone for the foundation of the house of Domine Megapolensis, graded the latter's garden and did other day labor. In Sept. 1648, he seems to have been in the employ of Teunis Dircksz van Vechten.

Jan Michielsz, from Edam, [province of North Holland]; was a tailor by trade and arrived by het Wapen van Noorwegen, accompanied by his young son, for whom the patroon paid one year's board to the Orphan Masters at Edam. April 30, 1648, the court of the colony granted the petition of Jan Verbeeck and Jan Michielsz to exercise their trade as tailors, with one helper, to the exclusion of all others. In 1651, Jan Michielsz built a small house in the village and agreed to pay eight beavers a year for ground rent and the right to exercise his trade.

Rijck (Rijckert) Rutgersz; was engaged for six years, beginning Aug. 16, 1638, at wages of f120 a year. From 1640 to 1644, he served under Teunis Dircksz van Vechten, with whom he would seem to have come on het Wapen van Noorwegen. He leased Bethlehem's Island, Nov. 29, 1648, for the term of six years, but left the island, March 17, 1650, perhaps as the result of a quarrel with Christoffel Davids, who struck him on the head with a club on March 3, 1650. Jan Reyersz, from Houten, succeeded him on the farm.

Abraham Stevensz, in the earliest accounts referred to as *Abraham Stevensz Jongen* (the boy), later as *Abraham Stevensz Croaet* (the Croatian), and in 1650 as *Abraham Stevensz d Capeteijn* (the captain); he is credited with six years' wages from Aug. 14, 1638, two years at f30 a year, two years at f40 a year, and two years at f50 a year; for 4½ years he served under Teunis Dircksz van Vechten. In 1646, he is referred to as *maet* (partner) of Claes Teunisz, alias Uylenspiegel. Abraham Stevensz leased the *Valeije* or maizeland, behind the farm of Broer Cornelis, Feb. 3, 1650, at an annual rent of one and a half beavers, taking upon himself all expenses; at Easter 1654, he turned the lease over to Barent Pietersz.

Teunis Dircksz van Vechten, presumably from Vechten, a small village near Utrecht; arrived with his wife, one child and two servants by het Wapen van Noorwegen, in 1638, but appears as early as July 20, 1632, as farmer on Pieter Bijlvelt's farm at the Manhatans. He is occasionally referred to as *Teunis Dircksen Poentie.* He worked in 1638 and 1639 as a farm laborer, but from 1640 to 1663, and perhaps later, occupied a farm at the south end of Greenbush, adjoining the farm at one time occupied by Teunis Cornelisz van Vechten and later by Cornelis Hendricksz van Nes. He had in 1648 and 1649 a half interest in the colony's brewery, in Greenbush, which was offered for sale on March 7, 1650. In Feb. 1651, he was prosecuted for calling Director van Slichtenhorst, in the presence of many people, *een ouwde graeuwe dief en schelm* (an old gray thief and a rascal); for calling Domine Megapolensis an informer and threatening to stab him with a knife; for selling his wheat at f11 a mudde, contrary to the orders of the patroon; for ordering Willem Menten four times during the night of Sept. 18, 1648, to fire off a musket in the brewery, thereby causing Monsr. Labatie and some soldiers of the fort to cross the river; for calling Teunis Cornelisz a thief and a rascal and striking him on the head for having leased the six morgens of his, Teunis Dircksz', farm which the authorities of the colony had reserved; for fighting with Pieter Hartgers and Abraham Staas; and for letting two horses stand in front of Jan Verbeeck's house, in severely cold weather, without cover or food.

Christoffel Davids, also referred to as *Kit davitsz;* according to his own statement, he was born in England and on Sept. 3, 1658, was 42 years of age (*Mortgages,.A,* p. 93, Albany county clerk's office). He appears first in the colony in 1638 and between 1642 and 1647 is various times credited with tobacco furnished to Arent van Curler and Antony de Hooges. Till stubble time 1649, he was with Crijn Cornelisz in possession of six morgens of land in Greenbush, and July 22, 1650, he leased the *Dominees*

Hoeck, on the west side of the river, opposite Papscanee Island, for six years, at an annual rent of f50, in addition to tithes, Christoffel Davids to build his own house and fences and the patroon to furnish the live stock. March 3, 1650, an action was brought against him for striking Rijck Rutgersz on the head, for beating his servant and for wounding Jan Dircksz, from Bremen.

1639

By de Liefde

Sailed from the Texel September 25, 1638; arrived at New Amsterdam, December 27, 1638

Willem Juriaensz, commonly referred to as *Willem Jeuriaensz Backer* (the baker), once, in 1646, as *Willem Jeuriaensz, alias Capitaijn,* and again, in 1650, as *Capiteijn* (captain). He made a contract with Kiliaen van Rensselaer, May 7, 1638, and sailed by "the ship of the West India Company," presumably de Liefde. He is credited from about 1641 to Oct. 8, 1647, with wages earned by baking on the farms of Symon Walichsz and Gerrit de Reux and on the farm called de Vlackte; also, in 1643, with boards furnished to various farmers, apparently from the sawmill of Carsten Carstensz, in which he may have had an interest. At first he probably worked with Harry Albertsz, baker, who sailed for Holland about April 1641. Willem Juriaensz was sentenced to banishment from the colony for various misdeeds on Feb. 4, 1644, and again on Aug. 29, 1647, for attacking de Hooges with a knife, but in each case respite was granted on condition that he refrain from molesting people. In 1650 new charges were brought against him and July 18, 1650, he was once more sentenced to banishment from the colony, the court resolving July 27, 1650, that he be brought in irons on board the yacht of Rutger Jacobsz and taken to the Manhatans. Aug. 4, 1650, he was released to settle his affairs, on promise that he would comply with the last sentence, but whether on account of his old age (in 1650 he is described as fully 70 years of age), or for other reasons, nothing more seems to have been done in the matter. Nov. 30, 1651, Willem Juriaensz declared that he refused to fulfil his contract with Jan van Hoesen, dated Jan. 30, 1650, and Jan. 18, 1652, the court gave Jan van Hoesen permission to occupy the *erf* (lot, or bakery) of Willem Juriaensz, on condition that the latter be allowed to dwell in his house as long as he lived *ofte de gelegenheijt presenteert* (or an opportunity for removing to another place presented itself). *Cf.* O'Callaghan, *History of New Netherland,* 1:437-38.

Jacob Aertsz (Arentsz), from Utrecht: referred to as *Jacob Aertsz Wagenaer,* and also as *Jacob Adriaensz Wagenaer* (the wagoner): sailed on den Calmer Sleutel, Dec. 1637, at the age of 25, as farm servant for Albert Andriesz. He served for 1¼ years at the Manhatans and June 26, 1639, began his service in the colony, for the term of six years, at wages ranging from f90 to f120 a year. He is charged in the accounts with supplies furnished by Albert Andriesz, but is entered as servant of Cornelis Maesen. April 2, 1648, the court ordered him to serve Evert Pels for one year, so as to complete his term. Feb. 23, 1649, he appeared before the court on the charge of having the preceding day, with Jacob Adriaensz Raedemaecker (wheelwright) and Harmen Bastiaensz, prevented Director van Slichtenhorst from arresting Jacob Toenijs, servant of Jan Verbeeck, in the *Greenen Bos.*

By den Harinck
Sailed from the Texel in May 1639; arrived at New Amsterdam, July 7, 1639

Jan Cornelisz, tobacco planter and carpenter, probably from Leyden; sailed by den Harinck in 1639; he is usually referred to as *Jan Cornelisz Timmerman* and appears to have been a master carpenter who had other carpenters in the colony in his employ. July 18, 1641, the patroon designates him as the person who may build the proposed church. His account runs from 1639 to 1647. In 1646 he offered to repair the mill dam on the fifth creek for f550, but his bid was thought too high and rejected.

Sander Leendertsz Glen; sailed with his wife, Catalijn Donckesz, by den Harinck, in 1639. March 11, 1649, they acknowledged their signatures to contracts of March 28, 1639, and Feb. 23, 1645, and stated that they sailed the two yachts of the patroon from 1641, for three years, "but not when they tapped liquor." The nature of the two contracts is not disclosed. Sander Leendertsz is credited with wine and beer furnished between 1644 and 1646, and charged with f32 a year from 1647 to 1652, for ground rent and the right to trade with the Indians. Aug. 2, 1649, Director van Slichtenhorst notified Sander Leendertsz and other skippers not to transport colonists to the Manhatans without his consent.

Andries Hendricksz; arrived by den Harinck and served for four years, beginning Aug. 14, 1639, under Cornelis Teunisz, from Breuckelen.

Marten Hendricksz, from Hamelwaerde [Hamelwörden, near Freiburg on the Elbe, Hanover]; came on den Harinck and was engaged for six years as farm hand at f100 a year, beginning Aug. 14, 1639. He was for three years and 8½ months employed by Michiel Jansz, and for two years and 3½ months by Cornelis Teunisz, from Breuckelen. From Nov. 1, 1645, to March 1, 1646, he was in the service of Antony de Hooges. He is credited with 26 weeks' board of Hans Vos, the court messenger, and in 1651 appears to have had an interest in the brewery, with Evert Pels. In 1657, he is referred to as *Marten de bier Craaker* and *Marten de bierkracker.* He is perhaps the same person as *Marten Hendricksz Verbeeck,* who on Feb. 1, 1652, obtained a lot next to Jacob Simonsz Klomp, the rent to commence Easter 1653.

Barent Pietersz Koijemans [Coeymans]; came by den Harinck and was engaged for six years, beginning Aug. 14, 1639, at f30 a year for the first two years, f40 for the next two years and f50 for the last two years. He worked for four years under Pieter Cornelisz, the millwright, and is in the accounts referred to as the latter's *jonghen* (boy). Early in Oct. 1645, Barent Pietersz and Jan Gerritsz entered into an agreement with de Hooges for sawing boards at the patroon's mill on the fifth creek; Oct. 11, 1646, the agreement was canceled and a new one entered into whereby the two men jointly took charge of the sawmill, and Jan Gerritsz alone of "both the mills" [sawmill and grist-mill?], the contract to last till the end of Jan Gerritsz' term of service. May 18, 1648, [perhaps the

date of Jan Gerritsz' death], Barent Pietersz and Rutger Jacobsz leased
the sawmill and grist-mill on the fifth creek, at an annual rent of f550.
From Dec. 14, 1648, to Dec. 14, 1654, the same men are charged with f125
a year for water rights of a sawmill on the fifth creek, which Rutger
Jacobsz took over from Andries de Vos. Dec. 14, 1654, the same water
rights were leased to Barent Pietersz and Teunis Cornelisz Spitsenberch
for f150 a year, and Aug. 3, 1656, the two men obtained permission to
erect a third mill on the fifth creek for which they are charged f100 a year,
from Aug. 1, 1657. After 1645, Barent Pietersz is sometimes referred to
as *Barent de Molenaer* (the miller). Jan. 19, 1651, he is called *swaeger*
(brother in law) of Andries de Vos. A brother by the name of Lucas
Pietersz is mentioned in the court proceedings in 1650.

Harry (Hendrick) Albertsz, from London, baker; his first accounts in
the colony run from 1639 to April 2, 1641. He then left for Holland and
in June 1642, at the age of 29 years, returned to the colony, on den
Houttuyn, accompanied by his wife Geertruyt Dries, from Doesburch,
[in the province of Gelderland]. June 7, 1642, he signed a contract with
the patroon for the place of ferrymaster. He died before April 11, 1650,
when the land formerly occupied by him was leased to Thomas Jansz. He
was succeeded as ferrymaster by Jacob Jansz Stol.

Reyer Stoffelsz, smith; was at New Amsterdam in 1638 and succeeded
Burger Jorisz as smith of Rensselaerswyck on Aug. 18, 1639. He does
not appear in the colony after 1647.

1640

By den Waterhondt
Sailed from the Texel in June or July 1640

Gijsje Berents [Barents], wife of Pieter Jacobsz; is charged with board
on den Waterhondt in 1640, and credited with 28 days' work done by her
husband on the house of Arent van Curler. It is not unlikely that her
husband was the same person as Pieter Jacobsz, *constapel* of Fort Orange,
who on April 15, 1652, by order of Johannes Dyckman tore van Slichtenhorst's proclamation from the house of Gijsbert Cornelisz, the tavern
keeper.

Adriaen Teunisz van der Bilt; was engaged for six years, beginning
Sept. 24, 1640, three years at f90 a year and three years at f100 a year.
He probably came by den Waterhondt, as farm laborer for Symon Walichsz.
It is uncertain whether the words *van der Bilt,* represent a family name,
or have reference to the village of de Bilt, near Utrecht, as Adriaen
Teunisz' place of origin. If used as a family name, it is probable that
Adriaen Teunisz van der Bilt was the same person as *Arijen Teunisz van
Luijten* [from Luyten-Ambacht, in North Brabant], who is charged with
supplies in 1642.

Lysbeth Brants, } daughters of Brant Peelen van Nykerck. They came
Gerritje Brants, } by den Waterhondt.

Cornelis Cornelisz, from Schoenderwoerdt [Schoonrewoerd, in the
province of South Holland]; served as farm laborer for six years, begin-

ning Sept. 4, 1640, at wages ranging from f80 to f100 a year. He is probably the same person as *Cornelis Vos*, and *Cornelis Cornelisz alias Vosje*, who appears in the account books from 1642 to 1657. Jan. 29, 1649, *Cornelis gen* *vossgen* (Cornelis, called vossgen) leases a farm adjoining Rem Jansz, the smith, on the north.

Jan Cornelisz, from Houten, [near Utrecht]; was engaged as farm hand for six years; three years at f100 a year and three years at f110 a year, his wages beginning Sept. 4, 1640. For the first year and eight months he was in the service of Symon Walichsz; the rest of his term he was in the service of Crijn Cornelisz, from Houten. He was probably a brother of Crijn Cornelisz and would seem to have come with him on den Waterhondt, in company with Cornelis Crijnen and Jan Crijnen.

Cornelis Crijnen (Krijnen, Quirijnen), from Houten, [near Utrecht]; is charged with board on den Waterhondt and credited with wages for mason's work on cellar of Domine Megapolensis and for spading of gardens. He was probably a son of Crijn Cornelisz, from Houten, whose surety he became July 7, 1646. Oct. 13, 1648, he was forbidden to leave the colony without furnishing two sureties for the payment of certain amounts owed by him, and April 29, 1649, he is referred to as having left the colony.

Jan Crijnen (Krijnen), from Houten, [near Utrecht]. Before Sept. 6, 1642, he was for a year and six months in the service of Symon Walichsz; after that date he appears to have been in the service of Crijn Cornelisz, from Houten. He was probably the latter's son and may have arrived with Cornelis Crijnen by den Waterhondt.

Claes Gerritsz, from Schoennerwoorde [Schoonrewoerd, in the province of South Holland]; was engaged as farm laborer May 26, 1640, for six years, three years at f100 a year and three years at f110 a year. His wages in the colony began Sept. 24, 1640. He was at different times employed by Brant Peelen, Michiel Jansz, Cornelis Teunisz, from Breuckelen, and on the farm called de Vlackte. In 1648, he was prosecuted by Director van Slichtenhorst for selling ammunition and bartering skins, contrary to his contract. Claes Gerritsz claimed that van Curler gave him permission to trade and the case dragged along till Nov. 10, 1651, when it was settled by arbitration.

Nijs Jacobsz; was engaged for six years, as farm hand, at wages ranging from f20 to f40 a year. His term of service began Sept. 4, 1640, and his board is charged to Crijn Cornelisz, from Houten; he doubtless came with the latter on den Waterhondt.

Teunis Jacobsz, from Schoonderwoert [Schoonrewoerd, in the province of South Holland]; in one instance referred to as *Tuenis Rut Jacobsz broeder* (Tuenis, the brother of Rutger Jacobsz); was engaged as farm hand for the term of six years, beginning Sept. 4, 1640; three years at f90 a year and three years at f100 a year. He served apparently first under Symon Walichsz and then under Cornelis Teunisz, from Breuckelen. He probably came by den Waterhondt. From 1650 to 1652 he is charged with f16 a year for a house lot. He married April 19, 1650, at New Amsterdam, Sara Denijs, from England.

Jan Reyersz, from Houten, [near Utrecht]; was engaged for six years, beginning Sept. 4, 1640, at wages of f105 a year for the first three years and of f112 a year for the last three years. He served for 1¾ years under Cornelis Maesen and for the rest of his term under Crijn Cornelisz, from Houten. March 17, 1650, he took over from Rijck Rutgersz the lease of Bethlehem's Island, which was renewed on Feb. 15, 1653, for eight years, at a yearly rent of f230 and f45 for tithes.

Dirck Teunisz, son of Teunis Dircksz van Vechten; came by den Waterhondt.

_____

Gerrit Jansz, from Haerlem; also referred to as *Gerrit Jansen Cuyper* and *Gerrit Jansz Kuijper* (the cooper); seems to have done cooper's work in the colony as early as 1640, and is mentioned in the court proceedings under date of July 16, 1648. May 4, 1647, Antony de Hooges gave him a promissory note for f28, being the balance of money due to him for *'thaelen vant Geschut* (bringing the ordnance).

Cornelis Spierinck; charged with supplies in 1642 and 1643 and credited with f107:15:8 for copying and other work in the service of Arent van Curler, in the course of 1½ years, previous to the arrival of Antony de Hooges in the spring of 1642.

1641

By den Eyckenboom

Sailed from Amsterdam, May 17, 1641; arrived at New Amsterdam in August 1641

Adriaen van der Donck, from Breda, [in the province of North Brabant]; son of Cornelis van der Donck, who appears in New Netherland in 1655. Adriaen van der Donck was commissioned officer of justice, or schout, of Rensselaerswyck, May 13, 1641, and sailed four days later by den Eyckenboom. He occupied a farm on Castle Island till Jan. 17, 1646, when the house was destroyed by fire and he and his wife, the daughter of the Rev. Francis Doughty, temporarily accepted the hospitality of Antony de Hooges. Feb. 23, after a quarrel with de Hooges, he left the latter's house and moved to the fort (*see* de Hooges' account of the quarrel, O'Callaghan, *History of New Netherland*, 1:469–70, erroneously attributed to van Curler, who was at the time in Holland). May 3, 1646, van der Donck was still in the colony, but soon after he left and established a sawmill and plantation on the *Saegh kil*, in his colony of Colendonck, in the present city of Yonkers, for which he had obtained a grant in 1645. Before leaving Rensselaerswyck, he transferred to Cornelis Segersz van Voorhout the remaining three years' lease of his farm on Castle Island. He was succeeded as officer by Nicolaes Coorn. Early in May 1646, in an account with Abraham Clock, de Hooges refers to van der Donck as *de Joncker*, which is probably the earliest mention of the title and which may have reference to his having recently become proprietor of a colony. Adriaen van der Donck died in 1655.

Cornelis Hendricksz van Nes (van Es); was in the colony in 1641, and probably came with Andries de Vos, on den Eyckenboom. From 1642, he is charged with tithes of a farm at Bethlehem, which he seems to have occupied till the fall of 1648, when van Slichtenhorst brought actions against him for calling him a liar and a cheat and for throwing oat straw on the dump heap out of spite against the director and to the detriment of the next lessee. In April 1649, he made preparations to leave the colony, but for some reason stayed and Aug. 25, 1650, he leased, for eight years at f225 a year, a farm in Greenbush, formerly occupied by Teunis Cornelisz van Vechten, together with six morgens of land belonging to the adjoining farm of Teunis Dircksz van Vechten. Van Nes served as *raets persoon* (councilor) of Rensselaerswyck, at an annual salary of f50, from 1652 to 1658, and again in 1660, 1661 and 1663. He lived with his wife Maijgen Hendricksen, at Vianen, province of South Holland, in 1625, and owned land at Scherperswyck, near Leksmond, in the neighborhood of Vianen, as late as 1661.

Andries de Vos; was a carpenter by trade and sailed by den Eyckenboom in May 1641. He occupied a farm [at Bethlehem?] from 1642 and in Oct. 1648 is referred to as *gerechts persoon* (member of the court). Jan. 21, 1649, the court of the colony decided that he must pay f62:10 a year for the patroon's rights of the mill at Bethlehem. Oct. 18, 1650, he entered into an agreement to lease the creek south of Thomas Chambers' farm for six years at an annual rent of f75 and to erect thereon a saw- and grist-mill, but Feb. 16, 1651, he was released from his obligation on the ground of inconvenience. He was a brother in law of Barent Pietersz Koijemans.

Hans Jansz Eencluys (een kluijs, in Cluijs), by his mark well identified with Hans Jansz, from Rotterdam; appears at New Amsterdam in 1639 and seems to have been in Rensselaerswyck as early as 1641. He was in July 1648, preparatory to Stuyvesant's visit, employed with Jan Dircksz, from Bremen, to clean the colony's cannon, and in the spring of 1650 acted as interpreter for Jacob Jansz Flodder in buying land from the Indians. In 1651 he operated a sawmill for Evert Pels, being under contract till May 1652. Nov. 3, 1651, Hans Jansz and Crijn Cornelisz received permission to erect a sawmill on a creek on the west side of the river, a little north of Beeren Island; Sept. 30, 1656, Hans Jansz and Abraham Pietersz Vosburch obtained a lease of the water power on the creek south of the farm of Jan Barentsz Wemp.

1642

By den Coninck David

Sailed from Amsterdam, July 23, 1641 ; arrived at New Amsterdam, November 29, 1641

Antony de Hooges; was engaged as underbookkeeper and assistant to Arent van Curler, and sailed from the Texel by den Coninck David, July 30, 1641. He reached New Amsterdam Nov. 29, 1641, but apparently did not arrive in the colony till April 10, 1642, being credited from that date till April 10, 1644, with a salary of f150 a year. From van Curler's departure for Holland, in Oct. 1644, till van Slichtenhorst's arrival on March 22, 1648, he was entrusted with the business management of the colony; from the latter date till his death, on or about Oct. 11, 1655, he held the offices of secretary and *gecommitteerde*. In the accounts, he is credited, from May 11, 1652, to Oct. 11, 1655, with a salary of f360 a year as secretary, and for the same period with a salary of f100 as *gecommitteerde*, also with f56, for salary as *voorleeser* (reader in the church) during two months and one week in 1653. In a petition for salary, March 27, 1648, he states that he has been for more than six years in the service of the patroon and for four years has not received any salary; that he has now been entrusted with a new office without any mention of salary; and that he must have a house built inasmuch as the storehouse, assigned to him for a dwelling, has been turned into a church. He married, in Oct. 1647, a daughter of Albert Andriesz, named Eva, who on Aug. 13, 1657, became the wife of Roelof Swartwout.

Lucas Smit (Smith, Smitt, Smits), from Jehansberg [Johannisburg, in the district of Gumbinnen, in East Frussia]; arrived at New Amsterdam, by den Coninck David, Nov. 29, 1641, and at once entered the service of Domine Bogardus. Aug. 13, 1642, he came to Rensselaerswyck and from that date till May 1, 1644, was employed at the patroon's house at wages of f100 a year. From May 1, 1644, to April 13, 1646, he served as a farm laborer on de Vlackte and also as a clerk, at a yearly salary of f200. He left the colony in 1646, with a testimonial of good conduct from Antony de Hooges.

Jan Teunisz, from Leyden, carpenter; sailed by den Coninck David at the end of July 1641, but does not appear in the colony till 1642. He left probably about 1646.

Jan Verbeeck, from Breda, [province of North Brabant], tailor; was to sail by den Coninck David with his wife, child and maid servant, but in the accounts of the colony is charged with passage of himself, wife and child only. His account begins in 1642; he probably spent the winter at the Manhatans. Oct. 22, 1648, he was indebted to the amount of f737:9:8, which he promised to pay promptly in five instalments on condition that the first year, 1649-50, he should be free from ground rent for his lot in the *bijeenwoninge* (village). He failed to fulfil his agreement and accordingly is charged with an annual rent of f32 from 1649. His house stood in Greenbush and was in 1658 taken over by Jan Baptist van Rensselaer. April 30, 1648, the court of Rensselaerswyck granted the petition of Jan Verbeeck and Jan Michielsz for the exclusive right to exercise their trade as tailors with one helper [Jacob Teunisz], at wages of 36 stivers a day each for themselves and 30 stivers a day for the helper. Jan Verbeeck was appointed *Gerechts persoon* (member of the court) of Rensselaerswyck on Jan. 5, 1651, and took the oath on Jan. 12th.

Volckert Hansz, after 1651 usually referred to as *Volckert Jansz*, and still later as *Volckert Janss Douw*. His name is first mentioned under date of April 27, 1642; in the harvest of 1647, he was employed on the Vlackte. From 1647 to 1649, he and Jan Thomasz are jointly charged with f32 a year for ground rent and the right to trade; from 1649 to 1652 Volckert Jansz is charged with f32 a year for his place *aenden berch* (on the hill) on which he built a house. From May 1, 1653, to May 1, 1658, Pieter Hartgers, Volckert Jansz and Jan Thomasz are charged jointly with an annual rent of f560 for a farm on Papscance Island, formerly occupied by Juriaen Bestval. Volckert Jansz and Jan Thomas bought this farm in 1658, for 950 beavers or f7600; and Oct. 12, 1694, Volckert Jansz settled his account for one half of the tithes till 1688. Jan. 24, 1664, the council of Rensselaerswyck passed a resolution annulling the purchase of land from the Indians, at Schodac, made by Volckert Jansz and Jan Thomasz without the consent of the colony. When notice of this resolution was served on them, they produced a patent from Stuyvesant, dated Nov. 3, 1663. In 1650, Volckert Jansz accompanied Arent van Curler on an embassy to the Maquaes.

By den Houttuyn
Sailed from the Texel in June 1642; arrived at New Amsterdam, August 4, 1642

Hendrick Andriesz (Driesz), from [Doesburch, province of Gelderland]; was the brother in law of Harry Albertsz and sailed with the latter on den Houttuyn, at the age of 21. He appears in the colony till 1651.

Juriaen Bestval (Bestvall, Bestivall, Westval, Westvael, Westvaelt, van Westvaele), from Luyderdorp [Leiderdorp, near Leyden]; came by den Houttuyn and drew wages in the colony from Aug. 13, 1642. In July 1644, he is referred to as servant of Michiel Jansz. Jan. 14, 1649, Juriaen Bestval and Jochem Kettelheym took over from Evert Pels the remaining term of the lease, till May 1, 1653, of the farm formerly occupied by Symon Walichsz; Oct. 8, 1651, Jochem Kettelheym was released from his obligations and Juriaen Bestval became solely responsible. This farm was on Papscanee Island and was leased from May 1, 1653, to May 1, 1658, by Pieter Hartgers, and in 1658 sold to Volckert Jansz and Jan Thomasz.

Johan Carstensz, from Barlt, [in the province of Schleswig-Holstein, Prussia]; came by den Houttuyn and drew wages in the colony from Aug. 13, 1642. In July 1644, he appears as servant of Michiel Jansz.

Jan Helmsz (Helms, Helmsen, Helmichsen, Helmes, Helmessen), from Barlt, [in the province of Schleswig-Holstein, Prussia]; also referred to as *Jan Helmsen alias Jan de Bock;* came by den Houttuyn and drew wages in the colony from Aug. 13, 1642. From about 1650 to 1658, he is charged with an annual rent of f445 for a farm at Bethlehem which he appears to have taken over from Jan Dircksz, from Bremen.

Claes Jansz, from Waelwijck, [about 14 miles west of Bois-le-Duc, in the province of North Brabant]; came by den Houttuyn in 1642 and was still in the colony in 1649.

Paulus Jansz, from Geertruydenbergh, [in the province of North Brabant]; came by den Houttuyn and appears in the accounts as *jongen* (boy) of Adriaen van der Donck, wages beginning Aug. 13, 1642.

Jochem Kettelheym (Kettelhuyn, Kettelheun, Kuttelheijm, Kuttelhuijn, Cuttelhuyn);came by den Houttuyn and served in the colony from Aug. 13, 1642, under Andries de Vos. From Sept. 20, 1646, to April 20, 1648, he was employed on de Vlackte, at wages of f120 a year. Jan. 14, 1649, Jochem Kettelheym and Juriaen Bestval took over from Evert Pels the lease of the farm formerly occupied by Symon Walichsz, till the expiration of said lease on May 1, 1653, at an annual rent of f560, but Oct. 8, 1651, Kettelheym was released from his obligations and Bestval became solely responsible. According to O'Callaghan, *History of New Netherland*, 1:451, Jochem Kettelheym came from *Cremyn* [Kremmin, near Stettin, Pomerania].

*Cornelis Lambertsz, from Doorn, [near Utrecht]; is given among those who were to sail with Domine Megapolensis on den Houttuyn in June 1642, but his name does not appear in the records of the colony. He probably remained at the Manhatans and soon thereafter died, as in the marriage records of the Reformed Dutch church of New York, under date of Sept. 4, 1644, is found the marriage of Wilhelm Bredenbent and Aeltje Braconie, widow of Corn. Lamberts.

Johannes Megapolensis, formerly minister at Schoorl and Bergen, [near Alkmaar, in the province of North Holland]; entered into a contract with Kiliaen van Rensselaer, April 6, 1642, to serve as preacher in the colony for the period of six years, at an annual salary of f1000 for the first three years and of f1200 for the last three years. He sailed with his wife and four children by den Houttuyn in June 1642 and served as pastor of the colony from Aug. 13, 1642, till the summer of 1649. For the entire period of his residence in the colony he appears to have lived in the *grenen bosch* (pine woods), on the east side of the river, and it is there, in his own house, that religious services were held till some time between 1646 and 1648, when the patroon's storehouse near Fort Orange was adapted to a church. The real name of Megapolensis was probably *Grootstadt;* Kieft, in a letter of Sept. 11, 1642, refers to him as *doe grootstedius,* and references are found in accounts kept by Jeremias van Rensselaer in 1656 to a surgeon by the name of *Mr. johannes grootstadt* who was not unlikely the son of Domine Megapolensis.

Juriaen Pauwelsen (Pouwelsen, Pauwesz, Poulisz), from Sleswyck [Schleswig]; came by den Houttuyn and began his service in the colony on Aug. 13, 1642. He is referred to as *Jeuriaen Poulisz Jongen* (boy), and in July 1644, as the servant of Michiel Jansz. He does not appear in the accounts after 1644.

Evert Pels, from Statijn, or Steltijn [Stettin, Pomerania]; was engaged as brewer for the term of six years, June 5, 1642, and sailed the same year by den Houttuyn with his wife and servant. Feb. 28, 1647, he leased the farm formerly occupied by Symon Walichsz, on Papscanee Island for six years, at f560 a year, but after building a new house and barns transferred the lease to Juriaen Bestval and Jochem Kettelheym, Jan. 14, 1649, and turned the property over on March 25, 1649. Nov. 18, 1649, he leased, jointly with Willem Fredericksz (Bout) the farm formerly occupied by Crijn Cornelisz, in Greenbush, for which he is charged in the accounts with an annual rent of f400, from May 1, 1649 till 1661 when he moved to the Esopus; the same day they also leased the saw- and grist-mill in Greenbush, formerly occupied by Jacob Jansz Flodder, for which he is charged with an annual rent of f125, from May 1, 1649, till May 1, 1658.

Abraham Staas (Staes, Staet, Staets), from Amsterdam, surgeon; entered into a contract with Kiliaen van Rensselaer, Feb. 1, 1642, to sail to the colony with his wife Trijntje Jochims and one servant, and to practice as surgeon for the period of six years from the date of his arrival, to the exclusion of all others. He sailed by den Houttuyn with one servant, but apparently without his wife. In the contract his age is given as 24; that of his wife as 19 years. Staas is credited in the accounts with various supplies furnished by him between 1642 and 1648, indicating that he was engaged in business besides practicing as a surgeon; also with f30 for salary as surgeon from Nov. 16, 1645, to Nov. 16, 1646; with f60 for salary as surgeon and work on de Vlackte till Nov. 1647; and with f20 for salary as surgeon till March 20, 1648. He is further credited with f58:6 for salary as *Raetspersoon* (councilor), from Feb. 5, 1643, to April 10, 1644, and with f400 for salary as *Presideerende* (presiding officer of the council) from April 10, 1644, to April 10, 1648. Sept. 9, 1649, Abraham Staas obtained a lot in the *byeenwooninge* (village), near the first creek,

On the terms of the freemen. In 1658, he owned a yacht and is referred to as *Capt. Staes.*

Hans Vos, from Baeden [Baden, Germany]; was engaged for six years, three years at f90 a year and three years at f100 a year. He sailed by den Houttuyn and began his service in the colony on Aug. 13, 1642. Soon after his arrival he was appointed *Gerechtsboode,* or *Steeboo,* (court messenger), for which in the accounts he is credited with an annual salary of f40 from Oct. 12, 1642, to May 12, 1648. In addition to this salary, he is credited with wages from Nov. 18, 1644, to May 18, 1648, at f110 a year. Before Dec. 17, 1648, he entered into a contract to serve Pieter de Boer for four months, and Dec. 23, 1648, he was reengaged as court messenger, for four months, at a salary equal to f50 a year and board, upon condition that he work two or three days each week for the director at f1 a day and in the morning fetch water, chop wood and spade the garden; for work done for Pieter de Boer he was to receive pay according to contract and for work done for others as much as he could get. From Jan. 1, 1650, to April 1, 1650, Hans Vos served as court messenger on a salary of f20 a month, and one day's work a week for the patroon without further compensation.

Joris Borrelingen (Borlingen), Englishman, servant of Crijn Cornelisz; is charged with supplies in 1642 and 1643.

Willem Fredericksz, from Leyden, *Vrij Timmerman* (free carpenter); after 1651, commonly referred to as *Willem Frederickss Bout,* or *Boudt;* is first charged with supplies in 1642. Between 1646 and 1648, he is credited with f80 "for making in the church a pulpit, the sounding board, a seat for the magistrates, one ditto for the deacons, a window with two lights, closing up a window and [building] therein a small closet, [making] a rail near the pulpit, with a corner seat and 9 benches." By the term "church" must be understood the patroon's storehouse, near Fort Orange, which according to de Hooges' petition for an increase of salary, dated March 27, 1648, had been turned into a church. Between 1648 and 1651, Willem Fredericksz is charged with f142:6 for passage of his wife and two children, as per account of Geertgen Mannix [Nannincks], showing that he must have married Geertje Nannincks shortly after the death of her third husband Claes Jansz Rust, the baker (*cf.* petition of Pieter Wolphertsz, guardian of children of Claes Jansz, Nov. 30, 1648, *N.Y.Col.Mss,* 4:422). Nov. 18, 1649, Willem Fredericksz and Evert Pels jointly leased the farm formerly occupied by Crijn Cornelisz and the mill formerly leased by Jacob Jansz Flodder. From 1650 to 1652 Willem Fredericksz is charged with an annual rent of f16 for a *hofstede* (house lot) on which he had built a house.

Andries Herbertsz (Herbert, Herberts, Herpertsz), referred to as *Andries Herbertsz alias Constapel, Andries Constapel* and in one instance as *de Constapel vande Vierblaes* (the gunner of the vuurblaas, a kind of frigate, built of fir or spruce, formerly used in Sweden). He was apparently not engaged for a definite term of years, but employed at different times to do garden work, cut and haul lumber, build fences, or work at the grist-mill. Between 1659 and 1662 he furnished the colony with brick and tiles from the kiln conveyed to him by Pieter Meusz. June 23, 1662, he was severely wounded in a tavern brawl by Seger Cornelisz, whom, in self defense, he mortally wounded with a knife. Andries Herbertsz died before Oct. 12, 1662. His wife was Annetje Juriaens, sister of Volkertje Juriaens, the wife of Jan Fransz van Hoesen.

Albert Jansz, from Amsterdam, carpenter; is charged with supplies in 1642, and on Aug. 7, 1644, credited with 19½ days' wages at 16 stivers a day for work done at the house of Domine Megapolensis.

Claes Jansz, from Breda, [province of North Brabant]; is charged with supplies in 1642, and is referred to as a boy in the service of Adriaen van der Donck. After van der Donck's departure in 1646, he was for one year employed by Cornelis Segersz van Voorhout. He is perhaps the same person as *Claes Jansz Smith,* who in July 1647 importuned de Hooges at the Manhatans for settlement of his account and who sailed for Holland by de Prinses, which was wrecked in Sept. 1647.

Jacob Jansz, from Noordstrandt, or Norstrandt [Nordstrand, an island off the coast of Schleswig]; appears first in 1642, when supplies furnished to him are charged to Cornelis Hendricksz van Nes. With others, he took the oath of fealty, Nov. 28, 1651.

Jan Pooy (Jehan Poeij); was furnished with supplies in 1642 and 1643 and is referred to as *Boetgesel van Rens'wyck,* that is, sailor of the colony's yacht Rensselaerswyck.

Claes Teunisz, referred to as *Claes Teunisz alias Uylenspiegel* and as *Claes Teunisz Uylenspiegel* (the wag, or joker); is credited with two years' wages in van Curler's time and with wages earned on de Vlackte, from April 10, 1645, to the fall of 1646; also with wages of his partner Thomas de Engelsman; and with various amounts for sweeping a chimney, finding horses, etc. Dec. 17, 1648, he was prosecuted for driving his horse too fast. He took over the farm of Jan Andriesz, Dec. 21, 1649, and was ordered to vacate it Sept. 9, 1650, for failure to improve it satisfactorily.

Teunis Teunisz, from Loenen, [province of Utrecht]; referred to as *Teunis de Metselaer* (the mason); built a chimney in van der Donck's house perhaps as early as 1642. Jointly with Jan Gouw, he contracted to build a brick house for Jeremias van Rensselaer, Sept. 8, 1659.

Claes Tijssen [Mathijsz]; is charged with supplies in 1642 and some time before 1648 appears to have been in the service of Evert Pels. June 23, 1650, the court ordered Director van Slichtenhorst to pay ƒ192 due to Claes Tijssen for wages earned on de Vlackte.

1643

Lucas Ellertsz (Luycas Elbertsen); appears but once in the records of the colony, under date of May 29, 1643, when his account is charged to Cornelis Teunisz, from Meerkerck. He was in New Amsterdam in June 1646 and in Beverwyck in 1661.

Jacob Jonasz; is charged under date of June 12, 1643, with 16 stivers and 4 pence for ¼ yard of duffel. No other reference to him is found in the records of the colony.

Wolf Nijssen (Wolphert Nys), from t'Stift, [bishopric of Utrecht]; bound himself at the Manhatans, June 15, 1643, to serve Evert Pels and his wife in Rensselaerswyck for two years, at wages of ƒ115 a year. After the expiration of his term of service, he was employed by de Hooges and others to sweep chimneys, cart hay, chop wood and do various other tasks. In 1646, or 1647, he was executed for a crime which is not named in the records.

Jan Barentsz Wemp, nicknamed *Poest;* appears to have been in the colony as early as 1643 and for a time to have served under Cornelis Teunisz, from Breuckelen. From April 10, 1645, to June 11, 1646, he had charge of the patroon's farm called de Vlackte and during that period is credited with wages at the rate of f300 a year, for the services of himself and his wife. He left de Vlackte June 11, 1646, on account of some *sporlingh met de wilden* (trouble with the Indians) and Aug. 13, 1646, agreed to take charge of the saw- and grist-mill on the fifth creek for the term of five years beginning July 25, 1646, at wages of f13 a month and f100 a year for board. March 20, 1647, with Andries Herbertsz, he took a lease of land south of Jan Dircksz, from Bremen, and east of Albert Andriesz, along the creek of Castle Island and the mill [Normans] kill, for six years, at an annual rent of f275 from Nov. 1, 1647. Andries Herbertsz, however, changed his plans and Jan Barentsz agreed to carry out the terms of the contract alone. He remained in possession of this farm till Nov. 1, 1654, when he took over the farm of Thomas Chambers, situated on the east side of the river on what later became known as the Poesten Kill. Jan Barentsz obtained a lot adjoining the stockade and north of Thomas Jansz, Feb. 1, 1652, the rent to begin at Easter 1653. In 1661, he owned a house which was leased by Jeremias van Rensselaer for the use of the schout, Gerard Swart. Jan Barentsz died between May 18 and June 28, 1663. His widow married Sweer Theunisz, from Velsen, [near Arnhem], who was engaged in Holland, Nov. 9, 1660, as a farm hand for Jan Barentsz.

1644

By het Wapen van Rensselaerswyck
Sailed from Amsterdam in September 1643; arrived at New Amsterdam in March 1644

Jacob Adriaensz, generally referred to as *Jacob Adriaensz Rademaecker* (wheelwright); probably the wheelwright from Hilversum, mentioned in the "Redress," of Sept. 5, 1643, as about to sail by het Wapen van Rensselaerswyck. He is charged in the accounts with rent for a small piece of land opposite the Mill Kill, seeded by him and Jacob Lambertsz in 1648 and also with rent, from 1650 to 1652, at f32 a year, for a house lot, north of Arent Andriesz, where he was to exercise his trade.

Claes Andriesz, from Hilversum, [in the Gooi, or Gooiland, province of North Holland]; hence also called *Claes Andriesz Gojer;* probably sailed on het Wapen van Rensselaerswyck, in Sept. 1643, and appears in March 1650 as servant of Jan Barentsz Wemp. March 26, 1650, he is sentenced for various misdemeanors.

Nicolaes Coorn; was commissioned by the patroon as commander and *commis* on Rensselaerssteyn, Aug. 26, 1643, and probably came by het Wapen van Rensselaerswyck. He succeeded Adriaen van der Donck as schout of the colony in the spring or summer of 1646 and apparently held that office till the arrival of Director van Slichtenhorst, March 22, 1648. In April 1648, in answer to a petition which has not been preserved, the council of the colony stated that his title was *Officier Luijtenant* and his salary f36 a month; also that he might style his tavern *Stadts Herberg* and build on site requested, but that consent could not be given to grant any one exclusive right to sell liquor. In 1648, he is several times ordered to render accounts of goods consigned to him by the late patroon and Jan. 27, 1649, he is summoned to appear before the court to prove that Hans Vos, the court messenger, is an informer, or else to retract abusive language used in the tavern respecting Hans Vos and the council. He seems to have left the colony in 1649. July 25, 1647, he gave a power of attorney to Claes Jansz Calff to receive property left him by his deceased mother Janneken Kassers, matron of the hospital at Steenbergen, [province of North Brabant] (*N.Y. Col.Mss*, 2:160).

Jan Dircksz, from Bremen, [Germany]; was commissioned skipper of the colony's yacht Rensselaerswyck on Aug. 25, 1643, when he would seem to have been in Amsterdam, though he had been in New Amsterdam as early as Aug. 4, 1639. From Sept. 14, 1648, to stubble time 1649, he occupied a farm at Bethlehem, which March 1, 1650, was leased to Jan Helms, for f445 a year. In 1651 he was in Catskill and Feb. 20, 1659, he conveyed his farm there to Eldert Gerbertsz Cruyf, in exchange for a house in Beverwyck.

Jacob Lambertsz van Dorlandt; was prosecuted in April 1648 for wounding Paulus Jansz Noorman, and in Dec. 1648 for calling Jochem Kettelheym an informer. He is apparently the same person as *Jacob Lambertsz Gojer* (from Gooiland, province of North Holland), who was prosecuted in Jan. 1651 for insults offered to Director van Slichtenhorst, de Hooges and Hans Vos, in Greenbush in Dec. 1650, and must probably also be identified with *Jacob schoenmaker* (shoemaker), to whom Evert Pels paid f20 wages in 1649, and with the shoemaker from Hilversum, mentioned in the "Redress" of Sept. 5, 1643, as about to sail by het Wapen van Rensselaerswyck. Jacob Lambertsz, from Hilversom, about 20 years of age, testified in regard to the burning of a house at New Amsterdam, March 9, 1644 (*N.Y.Col.Mss*, 2:99).

Jan Gerritsz, carpenter; is credited, under date of 1646, with 1½ years' wages at f90 a year, from March 26, 1644, to Sept. 26, 1645; with wages at f16 a month at the mill on the fifth creek, from Sept. 26, 1645, to Aug. 26, 1646; and, jointly with Barent Pietersz, with sawing of 2089 boards, at 3 stivers a cut, the last item presumably according to agreement of Oct. 1645 with de Hooges. Oct. 11, 1646, *Jan Gerritsz Timmerman* and *Baerent Pietersz* entered into a new agreement with de Hooges whereby the first two men jointly took charge of the sawmill, and Jan Gerritsz alone of "both the mills" [sawmill and grist-mill?], at f125 a year for board and 3 stivers per cut for sawing, the contract to last till the end of Jan Gerritsz' term of service. Jan Gerritsz probably arrived on het Wapen van Rensselaerswyck and died before March 17, 1650, perhaps as early as Dec. 14, 1648.

Dirck Hendricksz, from Hilversum, [in Gooiland, province of North Holland]; also referred to as *Dirck de Gojer;* was probably one of the four men from Hilversum mentioned in the "Redress" of Sept. 5, 1643, as about to sail by het Wapen van Rensselaerswyck. June 8, 1649, he and Claes Andriesz, from Hilversum, were ordered to complete the term of service for which they had been engaged and June 14, 1649, Dirck Hendricksz was taken over by Christoffel Davids. About 1652 he was at Catskill.

Jan Huybertsz, tailor; is charged with f50 for board on het Wapen van Rensselaerswyck in 1643, and credited with f29 for a suit of clothes made for Pieter Wynkoop.

Claes Cornelisz van Voorhout, second son of Cornelis Segersz van Voorhout; also called Claes Segersz, to distinguish him from Claes Cornelisz, the brother of Gijsbert Cornelisz, op den Hoogenberch. He occupied a farm on Papscanee Island from 1648 to 1658.

Cornelis Cornelisz van Voorhout, eldest son of Cornelis Segersz van Voorhout; is charged from Jan. 31, 1652, to Jan. 31, 1658, with an annual rent of f100, apparently for six morgens of land in Greenbush, formerly occupied by Christoffel Davids, which were leased to Teunis Dircksz van Vechten, on Jan. 31, 1650, and would seem to have been occupied by Cornelis Cornelisz after that year. In Jan. 1651, he is summoned to appear before the court to answer various charges of assault and battery. This Cornelis Cornelisz is probably the same person as *jonge Cornelis seegersen,* and *jonge kees,* mentioned in various accounts in 1656 and 1657.

Cornelis Segersz (Zegersz) van Voorhout; in his contract with the patroon, Aug. 25, 1643, referred to as *Cornelis Segertsen van egmont.* Voorhout is a small place near Leyden; Egmont lies near Alkmaar. He sailed by het Wapen van Rensselaerswyck with his wife, Brechtje Jacobs, 45 years of age, and six children, Cornelis, 22; Claes, 20; Seger, 14; Lysbeth, 16; Jannetje, 10; and Neeltje, 8 years of age. On his arrival in the colony, he entered upon the farm formerly occupied by Brant Peelen, deceased, which was one of the two farms on Castle Island; in 1646, he took over from Adriaen van der Donck the other farm for the remaining three years of the lease, and thus came into possession of the entire island In an undated will, recorded between 1643 and 1648, Cornelis Segersz and his wife declare that they possess nothing; that any property which they may acquire shall go to the five children who live with them; and that the sixth child, Lysbeth, who is married, and therefore does not assist them in the acquisition of property, shall receive as an acknowledgment one pound Flemish. At the time the will appears to have been drawn, Lysbeth was married to Gijsbert Cornelisz, from Weesp, the tavern keeper. Shortly after his death, in 1653 or 1654, she married François Boon.

Seger Cornelisz van Voorhout, third son of Cornelis Segersz van Voorhout and husband of Jannetje Teunis, daughter of Teunis Dircksz van Vechten. He died June 24, 1662, of a knife wound inflicted the day before at the tavern of Anthonis Jansz by Andries Herbertsz Constapel, whom he had severely wounded on the head with a piece of wood.

Abraham Clock; was a carpenter and perhaps also a mason by trade and is credited in the accounts with various amounts for work done between 1644 and 1646, notably on the house of Adriaen van der Donck on Castle Island, which burned down in Jan. 1646.

Gijsbert Cornelisz, from Weesp, [near Amsterdam]; commonly referred to as *Gijsbert Cornelisz waert,* or *weert* (tavern keeper). He appears at New Amsterdam as early as June 1639, and in 1646 is credited with wine and beer furnished at the departure of Arent van Curler, showing that he must have been in the colony of Rensselaerswyck in the fall of 1644. He is charged from 1647 to 1652 with f32 a year for right of the fur trade and with f40 a year for license to sell liquor. He married Lysbeth, the daughter of Cornelis Segersz van Voorhout, and died between Oct. 25, 1653, and Aug. 22, 1654. Aug. 24, 1654, Antony de Hooges gives a promissory note to François Boon, husband and guardian of Lysbeth Cornelis, formerly widow of *Gijsbert Cornelis: Ouwerkerck*, deceased, for wine and beer consumed at public leasings of farms, communion service, in household of patroon, etc. Ouwerkerck, or Oudekerk, is a small place on the river Amstel, a few miles west of Weesp.

Pieter Hartgers (Hartgars, Hartgras, Harties, Hartiens, Hertgers); signs his name *Pieter hartgerts*. He is credited in the accounts with a salary of f14 a month, from Nov. 1, 1644, to Feb. 1, 1648, and during this period, which closely corresponds to that of van Curler's absence, appears to have assisted de Hooges in the management of the colony. From 1647 to 1652, he is charged with f32 a year for ground rent and the right to trade, and as early as 1646 he seems to have had a brewery. May 4, 1649, he and de Hooges leased for three years a garden between Fort Orange and the patroon's *hof*, where formerly the patroon's trading house stood, and about the same time Pieter Hartgers agreed to pay an annual rent, beginning in 1653, of four beavers for a lot for his mother in law *Annetjen Dom* [Annetje Jans, widow of Domine Bogardus] on which he built a house. From May 1, 1653, to May 1, 1658, Pieter Hartgers, Volckert Jansz and Jan Thomasz were joint lessees of a farm on Papscanee Island, formerly occupied by Juriaen Bestval. Pieter Hartgers was at Amsterdam Dec. 20, 1660, and made an agreement with Jan Baptist van Rensselaer, regarding the purchase of 30 pieces of duffel which were to be delivered to him on his return to Fort Orange.

Mathijs Jansz; is credited in the accounts with wages for baking at the house of the patroon and with beer furnished between 1644 and 1646. He died before Oct. 13, 1648.

Jan Thomasz; is first mentioned about 1644, and in 1646 is referred to as the former servant of Adriaen van der Donck. June 11, 1646, while de Hooges was at the Manhatans, he was engaged by Pieter Hartgers as farmer on de Vlackte, in place of Jan Barentsz Wemp, at yearly wages of f250, cloth for a suit, one pair of shoes and two shirts. March 25, 1649, Director van Slichtenhorst ended his contract. In 1648 he had a house built by Thomas Chambers and from 1653 to 1658 he, Pieter Hartgers and Volckert Jansz appear as lessees of the farm on Papscanee Island formerly occupied by Juriaen Bestval. He bought this farm, jointly with Volckert Jansz, in 1658 and continued to pay tithes till 1684, from which date till 1688 tithes were paid by his widow. With Volckert Jansz he obtained a patent for land at Schodac in 1663.

Adriaen Willemsz; was sentenced to banishment from the colony, Aug. 13, 1644, for having stolen some beaver skins from the house of Arent van Curler.

1645

Richard Briggom [Brigham?], Englishman; was employed by Antony de Hooges, from 1645 to 1647, in chopping wood, cooking, spading and similar work. In 1646 his wages are credited to Sander Leendertsz.

Jacob Jansz Stol; signs himself *Jacob Jansz Hap;* appears first in the accounts of the colony under date of 1645 and in that year furnished various colonists with shoes, stockings, shirts and other supplies. He acted as skipper between Rensselaerswyck and New Amsterdam in July 1649, and soon after succeeded Harry Albertsz, from London, as ferrymaster of the colony. Feb. 15, 1652, he accompanied Johannes Dyckman in serving on the authorities of the colony an extract from the resolutions of the director general and council of Jan. 29, 1651, and a reply to the request for restitution of the colony's cannon. In 1658, he lived at the Esopus where with Evert Pels he had bought land in 1654.

1646

Rutger Adriaensz, tailor, brother of Gijsbert Adriaensz, from Bunnick; apparently employed by Jan Michielsz. He does not appear in records of the colony after Oct. 1651.

Thomas Chambers (Chamber), carpenter; appears first in the accounts in 1646, in connection with building a kitchen and chimney at the house of Domine Megapolensis. Sept. 7, 1646, he entered into an agreement about the lease of the land between the Wynants and Poesten Kills, in the southern part of the present city of Troy, for the term of five years, from Nov. 1, 1647. He occupied this land till July 1654 and shortly after moved to the Esopus. Sept. 23, 1650, he was chosen to accompany Arent van Curler to the Maquaes to renew the former covenant of friendship. He was nicknamed *Clabbordt*, a corruption of the English term clapboard, and may have introduced into the colony the method of weatherboarding houses with clapboards, which is not practiced in Holland.

Barent Gerritsz; worked, apparently in 1646, for seven and a half months on the farm called de Vlackte.

Jacob Hevingh (Hevick); was employed on de Vlackte from the harvest of 1646 till May 1, 1647, and thereafter did a variety of work such as helping to erect a new barn, hauling lumber, carting hops, etc. From March 3, 1649, to 1655, he is charged with f20 a year for a house lot and garden opposite Castle Island. In Dec. 1649 he was prosecuted for stealing some boards. He owned a house and brewhouse which about 1655 were sold at public auction and after passing through several hands were bought on Feb. 19, 1655, by Adriaen Jansz, from Leyden.

Jan de Neger (the negro); is credited in 1646 with f35 advanced by him for clothes which he was to receive in the service of the patroon, and in 1646, or 1647, with f38 *Voor dat hij hem heeft Laetten gebruijcken tot scherp Rechter, ter executie van Justitie, over den misdadiger Wolf Nijssen* (for having consented to act as executioner to carry out the sentence upon the criminal, Wolf Nijssen). O'Callaghan, in his *History of New Netherland*, 1:320 and 441, refers to him as the " hangman " of the colony. The wording of the entry in the account clearly shows that no such office existed and that the execution of Wolf Nijssen was an exceptional case, in which the negro was induced to serve.

Jan Fransz van Hoesen (Hoesem); was apparently in the colony as early as 1646, and in 1648 helped to erect a new barn for Jan Barentsz Wemp. By resolution of April 1, 1650, a garden was assigned to him between the first and second creeks and Jan. 18, 1652, he was given the use of the place of Willem Juriaensz, the baker, on condition that he let said Willem stay in his house "as long as. he lives, or opportunity offers." His wife was Volkertje Juriaens.

Thomas Higgins (Higgens, Higges, Heggens), referred to as *Thomas Higgins alias Compeer, tomas Compeer engelsman* and *Kleyne Thomas alias Compeer;* worked on de Vlackte in 1647, and about the same time appears to have been in the employ of Thomas Chambers. About 1650 he seems to have moved to Catskill. April 28, 1657, he entered into a contract for the use of two horses, for the period of six years. Perhaps he is the same as *Thomas de Engelsman,* who about 1646 is referred to as *maet* (partner) of Claes Teunisz Uylenspiegel.

Willem Leendertsz, referred to as *Willem leenertsz geelgieter,* and *Willem de geelgietter* (the brass founder); is credited with f150 for wages earned on de Vlackte, from July 1, 1647, to May 1, 1648, and charged with grain in 1649 and beer in 1654. He may have been in the colony as early as 1646.

Carsten Pietersz; came before 1646, being in that year referred to as the deceased *maet* (partner) of Jacob Hevick.

Jan Willemsz Schut (Schuth); was a cooper by trade and appears first in the accounts under date of 1646. He was to have sailed by den Harinck in Sept. 1637, but for some reason failed to go and Frans Altersz, the cooper, came in his stead. In 1657, appears at Beverwyck Willem Jansz Schut, alias *Dommelaer* (the dozer), who was probably a son of Jan Willemsz Schut.

1647

Harmen Bastiansz; appears first in the accounts of the colony in 1647, but was in New Netherland as early as Sept. 13, 1639, when with Evert Evertsz Bischop and Sibout Claesz he leased a sawmill on Nooten Island, now Governor's Island. He was a carpenter and with Dirck Jansz [Croon], built a house in Beverwyck on the site of the present National Commercial Bank, which he seems to have occupied from 1650 to 1652 and which on Jan. 25, 1652, was transferred to the name of Dirck Jansz. Feb. 9, 1652, Director van Slichtenhorst promised him indemnity for any loss he might incur by proceeding with the building of his house contrary to the orders of Johannes Dyckman. Harmen Bastiansz was in 1667 surveyor of Albany; Pearson and other writers refer to him as Harmen Bastiaensz Visser.

Thomas Coningh (Coninck, Cuningh, Keuningh); is credited with f14 for seven days' service on the occasion of the wedding of Antony de Hooges, in Oct. 1647, and appears among those who took the oath of fealty, Nov. 28, 1651. Feb. 19, 1655, he sold to Adriaen Jansz, from Leyden, a house, brewhouse, pigpen and fence, which he had acquired from Juriaen Teunisz on Feb. 1, 1655, and which formerly belonged to Jacob

Hevick. March 18, 1649, Cornelis Segersz engaged a boy of Thomas Coningh to help him in the harvest. Thomas Coningh is doubtless the same person as *tomas de Conine*, who married Marritjen Frans, from Beets, [province of Friesland], at New Amsterdam, Sept. 22, 1639.

Simon de Groot; April 10, 1647, Jan Michielsz is credited with f.28, paid to Simon de Groot for work done at the farm called de Vlackte. He is probably the same person as Symon Symonsz Groot, who went to the Esopus in 1662.

Marten Harmensz; received a lot in the *byeenwooninge* (village) and agreed not to trade with private traders, Jan. 12, 1651. He is perhaps the same person as *Marten de metselaer* (the mason), who is mentioned as early as May 25, 1647.

Claes Kalf [Claes Jansz Calff]; appears to have been in the colony about 1647, when de Hooges charges his boy Mathaeus with two pairs of shoes from Claes Kalf. He was a son in law of Brant Peelen.

1648

Jan Andriesz, from Dublin; testified Jan. 20, 1651, as to the killing of a cow and a horse of Thomas Chambers by the Indians in 1648 and 1649. He received a lease of a new farm, to be established north of *de Steene hoeck*, for the term of 6 years, beginning Sept. 1, 1649, but Dec. 21, 1649, the lease was transferred to Claes Teunisz. In 1656, he lived at Catskill and Feb. 20, 1659, a farm at Catskill, sold by him to Jan Dircksz, from Bremen, was conveyed by the latter to Eldert Gerbertsz Cruyf.

Gijsbert Cornelisz, from Breuckelen, [near Utrecht]; farmer on the farm called de Hoogeberch, hence frequently referred to as *Gijsbert Cornelisz van den Hoogenberch, op den Hoogenberch*, or *aen den Berch*. He is charged in the accounts of the colony with an annual rent of f300 from 1648 to 1653, and with an annual rent of f350 and tithes from May 1, 1653, to May 1, 1675.

Aert Jacobsz; occupied, apparently as early as 1648, a farm at Bethlehem which was destroyed by fire before May 1654. He then leased for 12 years a farm in Greenbush, north of Cornelis Hendricksz van Nes. About 1661 he moved to the Esopus.

Cornelis Jansz; is first mentioned in the court records under date of Sept. 9, 1648, in connection with the purchase of a musket belonging to the inventoried effects of the farm formerly used by Crijn Cornelisz. Aug. 2, 1649, Director van Slichtenhorst notified him and other skippers not to transport colonists out of the colony without his consent.

Evert Jansz, tailor; Oct. 13, 1648, the court of Rensselaerswyck granted *Evert Jansz Cleermaecker* (tailor), living on the island of Manhatans, permission to move to the colony and to exercise his trade, on condition that he build a house at his own expense. Nov. 7, 1651, he obtained a lot next to that of Abraham Pietersz, opposite the garden of Sander Leendertsz, being lot No. 2, on condition that he enter into a contract like other settlers and build a house at least two boards long. He was at New Amsterdam as early as Feb. 1643.

Jacob Jansz, from Stoutenburch, [near Amersfoort, in the province of Utrecht]; is mentioned in the court proceedings as farmer on de Vlackte under date of June 18, 1648, though Jan Thomasz' contract as farmer was not ended by van Slichtenhorst till March 25, 1649. May 5, 1649, he took over the lease of the farm on the terms granted to Arent van Curler, in Holland, Sept. 30, 1647, with property valued at f1426.

Paulus Jansz, referred to as *Paulus Jansz Noorman* and *Poulus de Noorman;* was wounded by Jacob Lambertsz van Dorlandt in 1648, and by Jacob Jansz Flodder in 1650.

Pieter Jansz, from Hoorn [province of North Holland]; also referred to as *Pieter Jansz de Boer,* and *Pieter de Boer* (the farmer); is first mentioned under date of Dec. 17, 1648, when Hans Vos is ordered to serve him for four months according to contract. He was still in Rensselaerswyck in 1666.

Jan Louwrensz, also referred to as *Jan Louwrensz Appel;* appears first in the colony under date of Oct. 12, 1648, as surety for Michiel Jansz. It is not unlikely that he was a relative of Adriaen Jansz, from Leyden, alias Appel.

Geertje Nannincks (Mannix, Nanninx); came with her son and little daughter by den Coninck David, in 1641. She was the widow of Tjerck Hendricksz and married, Dec. 28, 1641, at New Amsterdam, Abel Reddenhasen; July 21, 1646, also at New Amsterdam, Claes Jansz Rust; and about 1648, apparently in the colony of Rensselaerswyck, Willem Fredericksz [Bout]. She is charged in the accounts of the colony, under date of 1642, with f142:6 for board of herself and two children on den Coninck David, which amount is transferred to the account of her husband Willem Fredericksz between 1648 and 1651.

Evert Nolden (Noldingh); received permission to establish himself as a schoolmaster by resolution of the court of the colony of April 30, 1648. Nov. 16, 1651, he was prosecuted for having crushed Adriaen Dircksz' nose with a pair of fire tongs. He seems to have left the colony in 1660.

Brant Aertsz van Slichtenhorst, from Nykerck, [province of Gelderland]. According to O'Callaghan, *History of New Netherland,* 2:69, van Slichtenhorst was appointed director of the colony Nov. 10, 1646, and sailed with his family and servants for Virginia Sept. 26, 1647. The records of the colony show that he arrived March 22, 1648, and held the office of director till July 24, 1652, when he was succeeded by Jan Baptist van Rensselaer. Between June 29, 1651, and July 24, 1652, van Slichtenhorst was most of the time at the Manhatans and J. B. van Rensselaer acted in his stead, for the first two months apparently in conjunction with Capt. Slijter. April 4, 1650, de Hooges complained to the council that Director van Slichtenhorst had thus far rendered no accounts. The director replied that *hy wel wat souwde ontfangen dan dat het Antonij de Hooges heeft opgesnapt* (that he would have received something if Antonij de Hooges had not gobbled it up). Van Slichtenhorst was still in the colony in July 1655 and lived in Holland in 1660.

Pieter Teunisz, from Brunswijck, [Germany]; is first mentioned under date of March 28, 1648, as having taken farm implements, houses and cattle, formerly used by him and Crijn Cornelisz, with him to Catskill. In 1652 and 1653, Pieter Teunisz and Jan Dircksz, from Bremen, were summoned to appear before the court to settle their accounts.

Paulus Thomasz; testified Feb. 1, 1652, that he, Jan Dircksz, from Bremen, Pieter Teunisz, Compeer and others entered upon lands at Catskill on condition that they be free from taxes for ten years.

Hendrick Jansz Westerkamp (Westercamp); received permission on April 2, 1648, to seek a living in the colony by day labor or otherwise and soon seems to have established himself as a baker. In accordance with a resolution of April 1, 1650, he was granted the garden between the first and second creeks formerly occupied by *Capitaijn* [Willem Juriaensz, the baker]. Westerkamp died before Jan. 17, 1655. His widow's name was Femmetje Alberts.

1649

Jacob de Brouwer; received apparently in 1649, permission to build on a *hofstee* (lot), next to *Mr. hogens* [de Hooges], for which, from 1650 to 1652, he is charged with a rent of f16 a year.

Egbert Doysz (Dojesz); servant of Sander Leendertsz Glen, mentioned in the court records of the colony under dates of April 3, 1649, and March 22, 1652.

Thomas Fairfax; was employed by Christoffel Davids in 1649 and 1650 and is referred to as a mason and an Englishman.

Huybert, servant of Andries de Vos; was wounded by *Poulijntje*, in the brewery, in 1649. He may be the same as Huybert Jansz, who is mentioned in the court proceedings under date of Dec. 11, 1651.

Frans Jacobsz; testified in 1649, being then 17 years of age, as to a fight which took place at midnight Oct. 20, 1649, in Greenbush, before the house of Evert Pels. He may be the same as *fransoijs jacobsen de bruijn,* referred to in an account of 1656, or perhaps as *Frans Jacobsz Coningh,* who was in the colony in 1657.

Adriaen Jansz, from Leyden; also referred to as *Adriaen Janssen van Leijden alias Appel;* appears in the records of the colony as early as 1649. Feb. 19, 1655, he bought from Thomas Coningh a house, brewhouse, pigpen and fence which on Feb. 1, 1655, were acquired by Thomas Coningh from Juriaen Teunisz and which had formerly been in the possession of Jacob Hevick. He was a tavern keeper in 1656. From May 1, 1655 to May 1, 1657, he is charged with an annual rent of f24 for a garden, formerly used by Jacob Hendricksz.

Paulus Jansz, from Gorcum [Gorinchem, in the province of South Holland]; testified on Jan. 26, 1651, as to the killing of a horse of Thomas Chambers by the Indians in 1649.

Steven Jansz, master carpenter; moved from the Manhatans to the colony in July 1649 with his wife and daughter, and immediately entered into a contract at wages of f20 a month, which were paid to him for two years. Jan. 18, 1651, he acknowledged that he had tapped beer at his house without license from Director van Slichtenhorst. Feb. 1, 1652, he obtained permission to occupy a lot next to Hendrick Reur, the rent to begin in 1653.

Jacques Meulewels; testified on March 4, 1649, before the court of Rensselaerswyck, that the servant of Sander Leendertsz had gone into the woods with a loaf of bread and brought Indians with six packs of skin to his master's house. No other reference to Meulewels is found and it is doutful whether he was a colonist.

Aert Otterspoor, also referred to as Aert aerntsz van Otterspoor; was at Bethlehem, in 1649, 1650 and 1651. He came probably from Otterspoor, in the province of Utrecht.

Tijs Pietersz; was ordered, July 31, 1649, to present himself within 24 hours at the house of Director van Slichtenhorst to receive orders where to go according to his contract. The same day, Broer Cornelis was notified not to harbor him.

Jacob Toenijs [Teunisz]; was employed by Jan Verbeeck, presumably as a tailor. Feb. 22, 1649, Director van Slichtenhorst attempted to arrest him in the greenen bos (pine woods), for abusive language to the director and assault on the director's son, but was prevented from doing so by Jacob Adriaensz Rademaecker and Jacob Adriaensz Wagenaer. Jacob Toenijs is probably the same as Cobus de snijer (the tailor), who is referred to in 1657, and may also be the same as Jacob Toenisz, from Tuijl, in Gelderland who married Hilletje Toenis, at New Amsterdam, March 29, 1658.

Jan (Johan, Johannes) van Twiller; referred to by Jeremias van Rensselaer as Neeff Jan van Twiller (cousin Jan van Twiller). He was probably a younger brother of Wouter van Twiller, or perhaps, of Aert Goossens van Twiller, who on July 26, 1663, executed in the colony a power of attorney to Mr Peel van Hennekela, schout at Nieukerck, to demand of his brother in law Aert Jansz, shoemaker at Nieukerck, an accounting of the estate of his deceased father Goossen van Twiller and his mother Emmeke. Jan van Twiller was one of the Gecommitteerden (commissioners) in the colony in 1649, and at that time boarded with van Slichtenhorst. From July 24, 1652, to July 24, 1657, he held the office of raedts persoon (councilor), at an annual salary of f50. He probably left the colony in 1657.

Abraham Pietersz Vosburgh (Vosburch, Vosbergen, Vosberghen); was in the colony in August 1649, and from Easter 1651 is charged with f16 a year for a house lot, north of the patroon's house. Sept. 30, 1656, he and Hans Jansz, from Rotterdam, jointly leased a mill on the creek south of the farm occupied by Jan Barentz Wemp, for six years, at f100 a year.

Gerrit (Gerardus) van Wencom; was assaulted by a Mahikan Indian at Bethlehem, Dec. 8, 1649, and Sept. 23, 1650, was chosen to go with others on an embassy to the Maquaes. He was still in the colony in 1653.

1650

Pieter Bronck; was at New Amsterdam in 1643 and would seem to have been a relative of Jonas Bronck, who was probably a Dane. He is charged from 1650 to 1652 with an annual rent of four beavers for a lot in the bijeenwoninge (village), on which he received permission to build. Sept. 7, 1651, the court granted him permission to erect a tavern near his house, the director having withdrawn his request that according to instructions from the guardians of the young patroon but two taverns be allowed.

Dirck Jansz [Croon, from Amsterdam]; was a carpenter by trade and, apparently in 1650, built with Harmen Bastiaensz a house in Beverwyck, which was transferred to his name Jan. 25, 1652, on condition that he enter into a contract with the authorities of the colony and pay the patroon's dues. He is entered in the accounts as *Dirck jansz timmerman,* but is well identified with Dirck Jansz Croon, from Amsterdam, who in 1655 became one of the magistrates of Beverwyck.

Tijs Evertsz; testified on Jan. 12, 1651, as to the insolence of Jacob Lambertsz to Director van Slichtenhorst, Oct. 9, 1650, on the farm called de Hoogeberch.

Wilhelmus Grasmeer, a son in law of Johannes Megapolensis; sailed from Holland shortly after April 16, 1650, and preached in the colony of Rensselaerswyck in 1650 and 1651. He returned to Holland in Nov. 1651. In the court proceedings of the colony, under date of Aug. 4, 1650, occurs what purports to be an extract from a letter from Wouter van Twiller to Gerrit Vastrick, asking him to enjoin Director van Slichtenhorst not to let Wilhelmus Grasmeer preach in the colony, because he had been forbidden to preach by the Classis of Alckmaer. The passage was read by Gerrit Vastrick and written down by Antony de Hooges, but was afterwards found not to agree with a copy furnished by Vastrick. Aug. 15, 1650, Vastrick refused to have a certified copy made and the authenticity of the extract was questioned.

Laurens (Louwris) Jansz; lived with his wife Stijntje Pieters on *'t goet* [farm on the fifth creek?] of Adriaen Huybertsz, in Jan. 1650. The same year a garden was granted to him north of the large garden of Sander Leendertsz, according to resolution of the court, dated April 1, 1650.

Rem (Remmer) Jansz, from Jewerden [Jeveren, or Jever, in Oldenburg], smith; was at New Amsterdam as early as 1638, and in 1643 owned land on Long Island. Early in May 1650, he obtained from the authorities of Rensselaerswyck a lease of a garden adjoining the churchyard, and is referred to as being an *Inwoonder int Fort Orangien* (inhabitant of Fort Orange).

Lucas Pietersz [Koijemans]; mentioned in the court proceedings of Rensselaerswyck under date of Jan. 1650, and is called the brother of Barent Pietersz [Koijemans], who came in 1639.

Thomas Sandersz (Sanders, Sandersen), from Amsterdam; was an early resident of New Amsterdam and came to the colony about July 13, 1650, when the court granted "*tomes Sanders . . . Smith,* living at or near the Manhatans," permission to settle in the *byeenwooninge* (village) to support himself by his trade. July 17, 1650, *Saertje Cornelis,* wife of *Thomas Sandersz Smith,* testified as to misdeeds of Willem Juriaensz, the baker. Thomas Sanders was a smith and occupied at the Manhatans some time before 1649 the *mallesmits berch* (crazy smith's hill), which may have derived its name from him (*cf.N.Y.Col.Mss,* 3:68; 4:235).

Jacob [Jansz] van Schermerhoorn; presumably from Schermerhorn, in the province of North Holland; was in Rensselaerswyck in 1650 and perhaps as early as 1648, Jan Barentsz Wemp being credited between those two dates with the price of 12 lb of nails, paid to *labbatie* and *schermerhoorn.*

Philip Pietersz Schuyler. According to O'Callaghan, *History of New Netherland,* 2:177, Philip Pietersz Schuyler came from Amsterdam to America in 1650, and married Dec. 22, 1650, Margareta van Slichtenhorst, daughter of the director of Rensselaerswyck. The earliest reference to him in the accounts of the colony is under date of 1652, when he is charged with a small amount for some old boards from the patroon's house. March 25, 1652, he testified that Dyckman had stated " that he [Schuyler] would not have his father in law long, and that he, Dyckman, had written information to that effect "; also that Dyckman had threatened to run him and Robbert Vastrick through when, on New Year's day 1652, they tried to prevent the soldiers from beating the son of Director van Slichtenhorst. In the court proceedings, in 1652, the name is spelled *Scheuler* and *Scheuller*, in the accounts, after 1655, the usual spellings are *Schuijler* and *Schuyler*.

Willem Jansz Stol (Stoll), cooper; is charged from 1650 to 1652 with ground rent of f16 a year for a lot granted to him in May 20, 1650. He married the widow of Claes Hendricksz and moved to the Esopus in 1661.

Jannitgen Tuenisz [Jannetje Teunis]; sailed by den Coninck David and is charged in the accounts of the colony, under date of 1642, with f16:2 for her passage and money in hand paid by patroon. She married at the Manhatans Dec. 22, 1641, Dirck Jansz [Croon], from Amsterdam, and Nov. 6, 1642, was sued by van der Donck for not fulfilling her contract with the patroon. She probably came to the colony with Croon about 1650.

Gerrit Vastrick; was one of the *Gecommitteerden* (commissioners) of the colony in 1650, and on Aug. 15, 1650, was suspended from his office till he had cleared himself of the accusation of having given out a false statement regarding Domine Wilhelmus Grasmeer. He was at New Amsterdam as early as July 16, 1644.

Jacob Waelingen, from Hoorn [province of North Holland]; was at New Amsterdam in Jan. 1639 and may have come to Rensselaerswyck at an early date, though his name does not occur till May 12, 1650, when he was about to leave the colony. Efforts were made to retain him by offering him a choice of several farms, but he declined to take any, stating that he had not been able to support his wife and children satisfactorily. Oct. 1, 1650, he received permission to move to the Manhatans. He obtained a patent for land near the Kil van Kol, Oct. 23, 1654, and died before Aug. 17, 1657, when his widow Trijntje Jacobs married Jacob Stoffelsz.

1651

Claes Cornelisz; mentioned in 1652 as the servant and brother of *Gijsbert aende berch* [Gijsbert Cornelisz, from Breuckelen].

Adriaen Dircksz, *van Bil,* [from 't Bildt, in Friesland?]. On the complaint of Thomas Chambers that he refused to stay with him and fulfil his contract of March 24, 1651, he was sentenced on Sept. 28, 1651, to two weeks' imprisonment and the payment of expenses incurred by Chambers in hiring another servant during his absence. At the request of friends, he was released on the seventh day on condition that he faithfully perform his service.

Reyer Elbertsz, from Breuckelen, [in the province of Utrecht]; appears with his wife Marritje Baerentsz in the records of the colony under date of Sept. 25, 1651, when they leased a small parcel of land between the third and fourth creeks for eight years, at f25 a year, the lease to run from Easter 1652. Jan. 25, 1652, the court granted him permission to make brick.

Gillis Fonda; about 1646, Pieter Hartgers advanced some money to Gillis, a boy in the service of Antony de Hooges, possibly Gillis Fonda; Oct. 19, 1651, the court gave Gillis Fonda permission to distil liquor *in't greenen bos* (Greenbush), in a house belonging to Evert Pels, next to the brewery, on condition that he enter into a contract as to the *Gerechticheijt* *vande Heeren Mrs.* (dues to the patroon and codirectors). Gillis Fonda is at a later period commonly referred to as *Gillis Douwes Fonda.* To judge from his name, he must have been a Frisian.

Albert Gerritsz, carpenter; was at his request granted a lot north of the house of Laurens Jansz, Nov. 7, 1651, the rent to begin at Easter 1652.

Casper Jacobsz; obtained a lease of a *hofstede* (house lot), in 1651. He was apparently a day laborer.

Adriaen Jansz, schoolmaster; appears first under date of Nov. 23, 1651, when the court, upon his petititon, granted him f50 towards the payment of his house rent. He came probably soon after Sept. 9, 1650, when the council of the colony, in response to a petition from the inhabitants for a competent schoolmaster, appointed Arent van Curler and Goossen Gerritsz trustees of a fund to be raised for the building of a school. He was still schoolmaster in Beverwyck in 1657, and may have been the same person as Adriaen Jansz Croon, who Aug. 20, 1660, was about to sail for Holland.

Claes Jansz, from Bockhoven, [near Bois-le-Duc, province of North Brabant]; also referred to as *Claes de Braebander.* In 1651 and 1652 he was summoned before the court for having, out of spite against Director van Slichtenhorst, caused his servant to haul wood for Hendrick Westerkamp and Lambert van Valckenburch, contrary to ordinances of Oct. 16, 1648, Nov. 23, 1651 and Dec. 18, 1651.

Jacob Simonsz Klomp; appears among those who took the oath of fealty to the patroon on Nov. 28, 1651. Feb. 1, 1652, he was granted a lot next to that of Steeven Jansz, the rent to begin at Easter 1653.

Jacob Luyersz (Luijersz); was in the colony before Oct. 19, 1651, being ordered on that day to fulfil the terms of his contract with Jochem, the baker. March 2, 1652, Claesje, the negro girl of Sander Leendertsz, testified that she had delivered some of the goods which she stole from her master to Jacob Luyersz, who promised to take her to the Manhatans and there get her a husband.

Adriaen Pietersz, from Alckmaer, [province of North Holland]; leased in 1651 a house, north of Fort Orange, which the authorities of the colony and Charles van Bruggen, *commis* of the fort, had been forced to allow an Indian, named *den uijl* (the owl) *alias stickstigeri*, to build, and which, being found a nuisance, was bought of said Indian by Mons'r Labatie with the consent of the court of Rensselaerswyck, Nov. 28, 1650.

Jan Baptist (Johan Baptista) van Rensselaer; was in the colony as early as June 29, 1651, and Oct. 18, 1651, at the earnest solicitation of the court consented to accept the office of *Gerechts Persoon* (member of the court), in place of Rutger Jacobsz, who had asked to be relieved of his duties. In the accounts he is credited with an annual salary of f1000 as director of the colony, from July 24, 1652, to Sept. 24, 1658, when he left for Holland, and also with f1083:7 for 13 months' salary, from June 29, 1651 to July 24, 1652, when van Slichtenhorst was most of the time at the Manhatans and van Rensselaer acted as director.

Hendrick Jansz Reur, from Munster, [Westphalia]; was appointed *Gerechts Boode* (court messenger), Aug. 18, 1651, at a salary of f100 per year, in addition to fees for summonses and arrests. Nov. 14, 1658, he complained that his salary was insufficient and the court fixed a rate of fees for serving summonses in the various districts of the colony. Feb. 1,

1652, he obtained permission to occupy a lot next to Juriaen Teunisz, the glazier, the rent to begin at Easter 1653. He died before Feb. 4, 1664, when his household effects were sold at auction.

Captain **Slijter** (Slijtter); is charged with f114 for 9½ weeks' board for himself and his son, at the house of Director van Slichtenhorst, by order of the codirectors of the colony, from June 27 to Sept. 2, 1651. During this period van Slichtenhorst was at the Manhatans and Capt. Slijter appears to have had the management of the colony in conjunction with Jan Baptist van Rensselaer. July 30, 1651, Capt. Slijter made an agreement with Gijsbert Cornelisz as to the tithes of the farm called de Hoogeberch.

Robbert Vastrick; is first mentioned under date of Jan. 11, 1652, when he became bail for Lucas, the brother in law of Jan Thomasz, and his partner Arijen. March 25, 1652, Philip Pietersz Schuyler and Robbert Vastrick testified as to Dyckman's threatening to run them through with his rapier when on New Year's day 1652 they tried to prevent soldiers from beating the son of Director van Slichtenhorst. He left the colony before Sept. 30, 1657.

Cornelis de Vries; his name occurs but once, under date of Sept. 28, 1651, when Willem Fredericksz asked that he be summoned before the court. He may have been an inhabitant of Fort Orange or a free trader and not a colonist.

Jochem Wesselsz, baker; petitioned, Sept. 28, 1651, for a place in the *byeenwooninge* (village) to support himself by baking and was granted a *hofsteede op de kil* (house lot on [Rutten?] kill) at an annual payment of f32 for the right to bake and to trade. Jan. 26, 1652, he was ordered to remove within eight days the wood pile and pigsty from the lot of Jan van Hoesen and to refrain from molesting him or his family.

1652

Jan Bastiaensz van Gutsenhoven; the first reference to him in the records of the colony is under date of Feb. 8, 1652, when he testified to Dyckman's appearance in the patroon's court, accompanied by an armed posse. He was apparently engaged in business and in some way seems to have been related to Wouter van Twiller, or to the latter's wife, Maria Momma. He died in the colony between April 3/13, 1666 and July 6/16, 1667.

Gideon Schaets; was engaged as minister of the colony of Rensselaerswyck, May 8, 1652, at an annual salary of f800, for the period of three years from the date of his arrival in the colony (O'Callaghan, *History of New Netherland*, 2:567–68). In the accounts he is charged with f300, which he received before his departure at Amsterdam; and credited with one year's salary at f800, from July 24, 1652, to July 24, 1653; with two years' salary at f1000 a year, from July 24, 1653, when it was found that Domine Schaets could not well support his *swaer huyshouden* (expensive household) on f800; and with two years' salary at f1300 a year and house rent, from July 24, 1655, to July 24, 1657, when he became minister of Fort Orange and the village of Beverwyck. He continued as pastor of the Dutch church at Albany till his death, Feb. 27, 1694.

Gerard Swart (Gerret Swardt); entered into a contract to serve as schout, or prosecuting officer, of Rensselaerswyck, at an annual salary of f400, April 24, 1652, and succeeded Brant van Slichtenhorst in that capacity, July 24, 1652. He acted as schout of the colony till 1665, when the courts of Rensselaerswyck and·· Albany were consolidated and he became sheriff of Albany. According to his contract, Swart was to proceed to the colony with his wife, maid and servant, and to occupy "the house in which the former minister [Megapolensis] lived, standing ın *'t grenen bosch."* The name of Swart's wife was Anthonia van Ryswyck.

Juriaen Teunisz, often referred to as *Juriaen de Glasemaecker* (the glazier) ; signs his name *Jure Jan tunsen tappen* and *Jure Jan tunsen van tappen.* Jan. 25, 1652, the court of Rensselaerswyck granted him a lot between Gijsbert Cornelisz, the tavern keeper, and the land of Thomas Jansz, the rent to begin at Easter 1652. He kept a tavern in 1659.

Lambert van Valckenburch; reference to him is found in the court proceedings of Rensselaerswyck under date of March 7, 1652, when Claes Jansz, from Bockhoven, is prosecuted for having his helper do some hauling for Lambert van Valckenburch, contrary to the ordinances of Oct. 16, 1648, Nov. 23, 1651, and Dec. 18, 1651. Lambert van Valckenburch was at New Amsterdam as early as Jan. 1644 and received a patent for land there, March 16, 1647. In 1652 he was probably an inhabitant of Fort Orange and not. a colonist of Rensselaerswyck.

Pieter Winne (Winnen); also referred to as *Pieter de Vlamingh* (the Fleming) ; charged in the accounts with an annual rent of f275 and tithes from stubble time 1652 till May 1, 1655, for a farm, apparently situated at Bethlehem, which on April 10. 1655, was taken over by Eldert Gerbertsz Cruyf; also with two years' rent of a sawmill, at f150 a year; and with two years' hire of two horses for the mill at f60 a year. He made a will, June 1, 1677 (*Notarial Papers,* 2:11–13, Albany County clerk's office), in which it is stated that he was born in the city of *Gent in Vlaenderen* and his wife, Tannetie Adams, in the city of *Leeuwaerden in Vrieslandt.*

1653

Johan de Hulter;was a participant in the colony of Rensselaerswyck and sailed with his family and a number of free colonists by the Graft, in May 1653 (*N.Y.Col.Mss,* 11 :78). March 7, 1654, he obtained a lease of a farm north of the fifth creek, for which he is charged an annual rent of f275 for four years. In the accounts he is also charged with f900 for the purchase of a tract of land which is not described, but which is probably the land conveyed to his wife by Jan Baptist van Rensselaer, Aug. 24, 1654, upon which she seems to have established a farm, a brickyard and a tile kiln, all of which were sold by her at auction on Nov. 7, 1655. Johan de Hulter was a member of the court of the colony in April 1655 and died before Aug. 7, 1658. Aug. 5, 1660, his widow Johanna, who was a daughter of Johannes de Laet, appears as the wife of Jeronimus Ebbingh.

1654

Eldert Gerbertsz Cruyf (Cruijff, Kruyf), from Hilversum, [in Gooiland, province of North Holland] ; also referred to as *Eldert de Goijer;* is charged from 1654 to 1658 with an annual rent of [two?] sawmills; from May 1, 1655, to May 1, 1658, with an annual rent of f275 for a farm formerly occupied by Pieter Winne; and from 1658 to 1671, with an annual rent of f100 for a mill, apparently at Bethlehem. Feb. 20, 1659, Jan Dircksz. from Bremen, conveyed to him his farm at Catskill in exchange for a house in Beverwyck. A brother of Eldert Gerbertsz Cruyf, by name of Cornelis Gerbertsz Cruyf, was living at Hilversum in 1661.

Teunis Cornelisz Spitsenberch (Spitsenbergh, Spitsenbergen, Spitsbergh, Spitsberghen, van Spitsbergen); signs his name *Teunis Cornelise spitsenberch.* He and Barent Pietersz Koijemans are from Dec. 14, 1654, to Dec. 14, 1657, charged with an annual rent of f150 for a mill on the fifth creek, and from Aug. 1, 1657, to Aug. 1, 1658, with f100 for water rights of another mill on the same creek which they were authorized to build on Aug. 3, 1656. Teunis Cornelisz Spitsenberch appears as a member of the court of Rensselaerswyck in 1658, 1660, 1661, and 1664. In 1656 mention is made of a *Catrijn jans spitbergen,* who may have been his wife.

Jeremias van Rensselaer; sailed from Holland by de Gelderse Blom, Aug. 4, 1654; returned to Holland by den Beer, Oct. 28, 1655, and sailed the second time from Amsterdam by den Otter, shortly after June 14, 1656. He succeeded his brother, Jan Baptist van Rensselaer as director of the colony, Sept. 24, 1658, and held that office till his death in 1674. According to his own statement in a letter to his mother, he married Maria, daughter of Oloff Stevensz van Cortlant, July 12, 1662; in the records of the Reformed Dutch Church of New York, his marriage is entered under date of April 27, 1662.

1655

Pieter Adriaensz, referred to as *Pieter Adriaensz alias Soogemackelyck* (so easy), and as *Pieter Macklick* (easy); was one of the tavern keepers in Rensselaerswyck whom the director general and council in 1656 ordered to be arrested and sent to New Amsterdam for refusing to pay the excise.

Dirck van Hamel; succeeded Antony de Hooges as secretary of the colony in Oct. 1655, and served as such till his death on July 2, 1660. June 5, 1660, Jeremias van Rensselaer writes to his brother Jan Baptist van Rensselaer that van Hamel is unfit for the office of secretary and very-fond of brandy; that last winter he was for two months unable to attend the meetings of the council; and that since the arrival of his wife he has been very ill, apparently the result of drinking. His wife was Sophia van Wyckersloot; shortly after van Hamel's death she married Anthony Toinel.

1656

Trijntje Claes; mentioned as a servant girl of Jan Baptist van Rensselaer in 1656.

Teunis Jacobsz, from Hamersvelt, [near Amersfoort, province of Utrecht]; entered June 14, 1656, into a contract with Jeremias van Rensselaer, at Amsterdam, Holland, to sail by den Otter, and to do farm work for the term of four years from the date of his arrival in the colony, at f80 a year and board. He is described in the contract as being a *boere knecht* (farm laborer) and 20 years of age.

1657

Tjerck Claesz; charged in the accounts with f32 for hire of a horse from May 1, 1657, to May 1, 1658.

Frans Jacobsz Coningh (Koningh); charged, May 1, 1658, with f24 for one year's rent of a garden which he took over from Adriaen Jansz Appel.

Breuckelen, Cornelis Teunisz van, see Schlick, Cornelius
 Anthonisz van
Briggom (Brigham), Richard, 35
Broeckhuysen, Maurits Jansz van, 10
Bronck, Pieter, 40
Brouwer, Jacob de, 39
Brunsteyn, Claes, from Straelsundt, 6
Brunswijck, see Teunisz, Pieter

Carstensz (Christensz, Christensen, Carsten, Noorman,
 10
Carstensz (Karstenssen, Kerstenssen), Hendrick, from
 Norden, 8
Carstensz, Johan, from Barlt, 27
Carstensz, see also Christensz
Chambers, Thomas, 35
Chierts, see Tyaerts
Christensz (Christensen, Kristensen), Andries, from
 Flecker, 6
Christensz, Christen, see Carstensz, Carsten
Claes, Trijntje, 46
Claesz, Claes, from Vlecker, 5
Claesz, Gijsbert, from Amsterdam, 10
Claesz (Niclaesz), Pieter, from Norden, 10
Claesz, Tjerck, 46
Clock, Abraham, 33
Coerlant, see Smit, Lucas
Coeymans, see Koijemans
Compeer, Thomas, see Higgins, Thomas
Coningh, Frans Jacobsz, 46
Coningh, Thomas, 36
Constapel, Andries, see Herbertsz, Andries
Coorn (Coren), Nicolaes, 31
Coren, see also Coorn, Nicolaes
Corler, see Curler
Cornelis, Broer, see Schlick, Cornelis Anthonisz van
Cornelisz, Adriaen, from Barsingerhorn, 18
Cornelisz, Claes, from Breuckelen, brother of Gijsbert
 Cornelisz, 42
Cornelisz, Cornelis (Vos), from Schoenderwoerdt, 22
Cornelisz, Crijn, from Houten, 10
Cornelisz, Gijsbert (van den Hoogenberch, or aen den
 Berch), from Breuckelen, 37
Cornelisz, Gijsbert (Waert), from Weesp, 33
Cornelisz, Jan, from Houten, 23
Cornelisz, Jan, from Leyden, 21
Cornelisz, Pieter, from Munnickendam, 11
Cornelisz, Roelof, from Houten, 11
Cornelisz, Teunis, see Spitsenberch, Teunis Cornelisz
Cornelisz, Teunis, see Vechten, Teunis Cornelisz van
Cremyn, see Kettelheym, Jochem
Crijnen, Cornelis, from Houten, 23

Crijnen, Jan, from Houten, 23
Cristensen, Cristen, see Carstensz, Carsten
Croon, Dirck Jansz, from Amsterdam, 40
Cruyf, Eldert Gebertsz, from Hilversum, 45
Curler, (Corlaer, Corler), Arent van, from Nykerck, 17
Cuttelhuyn, see Kettelheym

Davids, Christoffel, 19
Dircksz, Adriaen, from Bil, 42
Dircksz, Jan, from Amersfoort, 18
Dircksz, Jan, from Bremen, 32
Dircksz, Teunis, see Vechten, Teunis Dircksz van
Donck, Adriaen van der, from Breda, 24
Dorlandt, Jacob Lambertsz van, 32
Douw, Volckert Jansz, see Hansz, Volckert
Doysz, Egbert, 39
Dries (Driesz), Hendrick, see Andriesz, Hendrick

Eencluys, Hans Jansz, from Rotterdam, 25
Elbertsz (Albertsz), Elbert, from Nykerck, 17
Elbertsz, Reyer, from Breuckelen, 42
Ellertsz (Elbertsen), Lucas, 30
Es, Cornelis Hendricksz van, see Nes, Cornelis
    Hendricksz van
Evertsz, Tijs, 41

Fairfax, Thomas, 39
Ferlyn, Jasper, see Gouw, Jasper Ferlyn van der
Flodder, Jacob Jansz, see Gardenier, Jacob Jansz
Fonda, Gillis Douwes, 42-43
Fredericksz, Hendrick, from Bunnick, 7
Fredericksz, Willem, from Leyden, 29

Gardenier (Flodder), Jacob Jansz, from Campen, 16
Gerbertsz, Eldert, see Cruyf, Eldert Gerbertsz
Gerritsz, Albert, 43
Gerritsz, Barent, 35
Gerritsz, Claes, from Schoennerwoorde, 23
Gerritsz, Goossen, from Westerbroeck, 11
Gerritsz, Jan, 32
Gerritsz (van Couwenhoven), Wolfert, from Amersfoort,
    5
Gerritsz, see Goverts
Ghijsbertsz (Ghysbertsz), see Gijsbertsz
Gijsbertsz, Claes, 18
Gijsbertsz, Lubbert, 8
Glen, Sander Leendertsz, 21
Gouw, Jasper Ferlyn van der, from Middelburgh, 6
Goverts (Gerritssz), Cornelis, from Flecker, 6
Goyversen (Goyverttsen), Jacob, from Flecker, 5
Grasmeer, Wilhelmus, 41
Groot, Simon de, 37

Gutsenhoven, Jan Bastiaensz van, 44

Hamel, Dirck van, 46
Hamelwaerde (Hamelwörden), see Hendricksz, Marten
Hamersvelt, see Jacobsz, Teunis
Hansz, Volckert, 26
Hap, Jacob Jansz, see Stol, Jacob Jansz
Harmensz, Marten, 37
Harmensz, Robert, 12
Hartgers (Hartgens), Pieter, 34
Havick, Jacob, see Hevingh, Jacob
Helmsz (Heling, Helms, Helmssen), Jan, 27
Hendricksz, Andries, 21
Hendricksz, Cornelis, see Nes, Cornelis Hendricksz van
Hendricksz, Dirck, from Hilversum, 32
Hendricksz, Gerrit, from Nykerck, 17
Hendricksz, Marten, from Hamelwaerde, 21
Hendricksz, Pieter, from Soest, 5
Hendricksz, Robbert, 8
Hendricksz, Rutger, from Soest, 5
Henypot, Symon Jansz, 18
Hebertsz (Herpertsz), Andries, 29
Hevingh (Havick, Hevick), Jacob, 35
Higgins (Higgens), Thomas, 36
Hoesen (Hoesem), Jan Fransz van, 36
Hogus, see Hooges
Hooges, Antony de, 25
Huijberts, see Huybertsz
Hulter, Johan de, 45
Huybert, 39
Huybertsz (Hubertsen, Huijbertsz), Adriaen, 12
Huybertsz, Jan, 33

Jacobsz, Aert, 37
Jacobsz, Casper, 43
Jacobsz, Cornelis, from Martensdyck, 7
Jacobsz, Frans, 39
Jacobsz, Jan, 8
Jacobsz, Nijs, 23
Jacobsz, Rutger, from Schoonderwoert, 12
Jacobsz, Teunis, from Hamersvelt, 46
Jacobsz, Teunis, from Schoonderwoert, 23
Jansz, Adriaen, 43
Jansz, Adriaen, from Leyden, 39
Jansz, Albert, from Amsterdam, 30
Jansz, Barent, from Desens or Esen, 6
Jansz, Claes, from Bockhoven, 43
Jansz, Claes, from Breda, 30
Jansz, Claes, from Naerden, see Ruyter, Claes Jansz
Jansz, Claes, from Nykerck, 12
Jansz, Claes, from Nykerck, 17
Jansz, Claes, from Waelwijck, 27

Jansz, Cornelis, 37
Jansz, Dirck, from Amsterdam, see Croon, Dirck Jansz
Jansz, Dirck, from Edam, 13
Jansz, Evert, 37
Jansz, Gerrit, from Haerlem, 24
Jansz, Hans, see Eencluys, Hans Jansz
Jansz, Hendrick, see Westerkamp, Hendrick Jansz
Jansz, Jacob, from Amsterdam, 13
Jansz, Jacob, from Campen, see Gardenier, Jacob Jansz
Jansz, Jacob, from Noordstrandt, 30
Jansz, Jacob, from Stoutenburch, 37
Jansz, Jacob, see Schermerhorn, Jacob Jansz van
Jansz, Jacob, see Stol, Jacob Jansz
Jansz, Jan, from Bremen, see Dircksz, Jan, from Bremen
Jansz, Laurens, 41
Jansz, Mathijs, 34
Jansz, Maurits, see Broeckhuysen, Maurits Jansz van
Jansz, Michiel, from Schrabbekercke, 18
Jansz, Paulus (Paulus de Noorman), 38
Jansz, Paulus, from Geertruydenbergh, 27
Jansz, Paulus, from Gorcum, 39
Jansz, Pieter, from Hoorn, 38
Jansz, Rem, from Jewerden, 41
Jansz, Roelof, from Masterland, 6
Jansz, Seger, from Nykerck, 6
Jansz, Steven, 39
Jansz, Symon, see Henypot, Symon Jansz
Jansz, Thomas, from Bunnick, 13
Jansz, Tunes, see Vechten, Teunis Dircksz van
Jansz, Volckert, see Hansz, Volckert
Jonasz, Jacob, 30
Jorisz, Burger, 15
Juriaensz, Willem, 20

Kalf, Claes, 37
Kettelheym (Kettelheun), Jochem, from Cremyn, 27
Klomp, Jacob Simonsz, 43
Koijemans (Coeymans), Barent Pietersz, 21
Koijemans (Coeymans), Lucas Pietersz, 41
Krijnen, see Crijnen
Kristensen, see Christensz

Labatie (Barije, Labatije, Labatje, Lebatje, Lebattij), Jean
    13-14
Lambertsz, Cornelis, from Doorn, 27
Lambertsz, Jacob, see Dorlandt, Jacob Lambertsz van
Laurensz (Loerens, Lourenssen), Laurens, from Coppen-
    hagen, 7
Laurensz, see also Louwrensz
Leendertsz, Willem, 36
Leyden, see Fredericksz, Willem; Jansz, Adriaen; Teunisz,
    Jan